Two Studies
in the Theology
of
Bonhoeffer

TWO STUDIES IN THE THEOLOGY OF BONHOEFFER

by

JÜRGEN MOLTMANN

and

JÜRGEN WEISSBACH

Introduction by Reginald H. Fuller

TRANSLATION BY
Reginald H. Fuller and Ilse Fuller

CHARLES SCRIBNER'S SONS · NEW YORK

CONTENTS

ABBREVIATIONS

Works by Dietrich Bonhoeffer

AB   *Act and Being* (New York: Harper & Row, 1961)-
Eng. trans., by Bernard Noble, of *Akt und Sein*
(Munich: Chr. Kaiser Verlag, 1956).

C   *Christology* (London: Collins, 1966). From *GS*,
Vol. III. Eng. trans. by John Bowden.

CD   *The Cost of Discipleship* (London: SCM Press,
1964)-Eng. trans., by Reginald H. Fuller, of
Nachfolge (Munich: Chr. Kaiser Verlag, 1964).

CF   *Creation and Fall* (New York: The Macmillan
Company, 1964)-Eng. trans., by John C. Fletcher,
of *Schöpfung und Fall* (Munich: Chr. Kaiser
Verlag, 1958).

CS   *Communion of Saints* (New York: Harper &
Row, 1961)-Eng. trans., by Ronald Gregor Smith,
of *Sanctorum Communio* (Munich: Chr. Kaiser
Verlag, 1960).

E   *Ethics* (New York: The Macmillan Company,
1955)-Eng. trans., by Neville Horton Smith, of
Ethik (Munich: Chr. Kaiser Verlag, 1949).

GS   *Gesammelte Schriften* (*Collected Works*), Vols.
I–IV (Munich: Chr. Kaiser Verlag, 1960).

LPP   *Letters and Papers from Prison* (New York: The
Macmillan Co., 1962)-Eng. Trans., by Reginald

H. Fuller, of *Widerstand und Ergebung* (Munich: Chr. Kaiser Verlag, 1949).

NRS   *No Rusty Swords* (London: Collins, 1965)-Excerpts from GS. Eng. trans. by Edwin H. Robinson and John Bowden.

Other Works

BevTh   *Beiheft zur evangelischen Theologie.*

Eng. trans.   English translation.

EvTh   *Evangelische Theologie.*

KuD   *Kerygma und Dogma.*

LCC   Library of Christian Classics, Vol. V (Philadelphia: The Westminster Press, 1961).

MW   *Mündige Welt*, Vols. I–IV (Munich: Chr. Kaiser Verlag, 1955–1963).

RGG   *Religion in Geschichte und Gegenwart*, 6 vols. (Tübingen: J. C. C. Mohr [Paul Siebeck]) (3d ed.; 1957–1962).

ThEx   *Theologische Existenz heute.*

WA   *Weimarer Ausgabe* (The Weimar edition of Luther's works, published by Herman Böhlen from 1883, and subsequently by successors).

WML   *Works of Martin Luther*. The Philadelphia edition, published by the Muhlenberg Press (1943 edition).

ZThK   *Zeitschrift für Theologie und Kirche.*

Introduction

BY REGINALD H. FULLER

In the summer of 1952—appropriately enough in the Austrian Alps—I was working on the translation of Bonhoeffer's *Letters and Papers from Prison.* I remember saying to myself again and again: "This stuff is dynamite." I hardly dared read it myself, let alone help to launch it on the English-speaking world. "How can Christ become the Lord, even of those with no religion? . . . What is religionless Christianity? . . . What is the significance of a Church (church, parish, preaching, Christian life) in a religionless world? . . . The 'beyond' of God is not that which is beyond our perceptive faculties. . . . God is the 'beyond' in the midst of life" (*LPP*, pp. 163–166). Or again, there was Bonhoeffer's charge against the later Barth for retreating into a "positive doctrine of Revelation": "Take it or leave it: Virgin Birth, Trinity or anything else, everything . . . has to be swallowed whole or not at all" (*LPP*, p. 168). Then there were those disconcerting observations about the world come of age, the insistence that integrity demanded our living in the world—before God!—*etsi deus non daretur* (*LPP*, p. 209). Or the apparently quixotic suggestion in the "Outline for a Book" that the church give away its endowments to the poor and that the clergy live off the offerings of the faithful or earn their living in a secular occupation (p. 239). And what about "being for others" just as Christ was the "Man for others" (pp. 237 f.)?

Next year the translation duly appeared. Generally the reviewers

11

treated it respectfully as an interesting piece of spiritual biography, particularly interesting in view of Bonhoeffer's ultimate fate. Here was the last will and testament of a twentieth-century martyr. For by 1953 the tragic circumstances of his end were familiar to the English-speaking world, at least the theological world, from G. Leibholz's memoir in the first work of Bonhoeffer's to be translated, *The Cost of Discipleship* (1948). One or two of the more perceptive reviewers found seminal thoughts in the letters. For instance, Charles C. West in *Theology* (January, 1954) wrote: "He [Bonhoeffer] has left to posterity a prospectus and a sense of direction which may well lead us beyond the conflicts of Barthian and liberal theology, and beyond the estrangement of Church and world." The theological world, however, for the time being continued on its own sweet way, still dominated by neo-orthodoxy and "revelational positivism." It took ten years for the dynamite to explode in Britain and America, and when the explosion came it was far more devastating than I had anticipated in the Alps in 1952. For in 1963 two books appeared which have radically transformed the whole theological scene. I refer of course to the Bishop of Woolwich's *Honest to God* and to Paul van Buren's *The Secular Meaning of the Gospel*. Each of these writers appealed to Bonhoeffer and in so doing put him on the map, at last, in the (English-speaking) world of theology and church—and indeed beyond.

Bishop Robinson acknowledged his debt to Bonhoeffer for two questions which the latter had asked in the *Letters*: 'What is Christ for us to-day?' and 'What is the place of worship and prayer in an entire absence of religion?' [1] In his answer to the first question, "What is Christ?" the Bishop takes Bonhoeffer's words "The Man for Others" as the title for his chapter on Christology. "The Man for Others" is enlisted as an alternative to "The Man from Heaven" (the orthodox doctrine of the incarnation). Under Bonhoeffer's banner Dr. Robinson elaborates a Christology of his own: "Jesus is the 'man for others', the one in whom Love has completely taken over, the one who is utterly open to and united with the Ground of his being." Then he claims: "It was some such Christology, I believe, towards which Bonhoeffer was working, and of

[1] John A. T. Robinson, *Honest to God* (Philadelphia: Westminster Press, 1963), pp. 75, 84.

which he left such tantalizing intimations behind him." [2] Whether this is a satisfactory Christology or not is irrelevant to our present concern. The question is, can such a Christology really claim the authority of Bonhoeffer? Is a liberal ethical humanitarianism the right intellectual context in which to place Bonhoeffer's phrase "the Man for Others"?

As for the second question, the place of worship and prayer in a religionless world, the Bishop works out his conception of "Holy Worldliness" independently of Bonhoeffer, though from time to time he does refer to the *Letters*.[3] All the way through, however, there is a basic difference between the Bishop's conception of the world and Bonhoeffer's. The Bishop regards the world as such, world *qua* world, as holy. The world as such is the place of encounter with God. Take for instance the discussion on "A 'non-religious' understanding of prayer." "We may begin," writes Dr. Robinson, "from the fact that people do give themselves to people. There is nothing religious about this. But to open oneself to another *unconditionally* in love is to be with him in the presence of God." [4] True, the Bishop occasionally inserts an appeal to some element in the New Testament proclamation: the world is "God's world for which Christ died." [5] But this is adduced as an additional proof of the intrinsic holiness of the secular, not as the crucial turning point in which God claimed the world for himself in Christ, a point at which the world became what it had not been before.[6]

Professor van Buren likewise takes as his starting point a question posed by Bonhoeffer, namely the "non-religious interpretation

[2] Robinson, *op. cit.*, p. 76.
[3] P. 85, n.1; p. 86 ("the beyond in the midst of life") and n.2; pp. 89, 90; p. 104, n.1 (citation of a passage on the nonreligious interpretation of "God" and on "the world come of age").
[4] Robinson, *op. cit.*, p. 99.
[5] Robinson, *op. cit.*, p. 87.
[6] The reader must not be led astray by the reference to the incarnation on the same page: "The Jewish priestly conception of the relation of the sacred to the secular was shattered by the incarnation when God declared all things holy." According to the Bishop of Woolwich it was only a false conception that was corrected by the incarnation; one religion was replaced by another. For Bonhoeffer, however, the world *became* holy as a result of the Christ event. The Lordship of Christ, dating from ascension, is for him the effective cause of the holiness of the world.

of Biblical concepts." But he, unlike the Bishop of Woolwich, is careful not to claim the support of Bonhoeffer for his answer: "Our method is one which never occurred to Bonhoeffer, but our interpretation may nevertheless serve to justify his hope." [7] And in his lecture at the Bonhoeffer colloquium held at Union Theological Seminary, New York City, on April 5, 1967, van Buren expressly disavowed any intention of posing as an interpreter of Bonhoeffer. Bonhoeffer had only stimulated him to ask certain questions; in no sense had he provided him with the answers.

Nevertheless, in *The Secular Meaning of the Gospel,* van Buren did refer on occasion to Bonhoeffer's letters. Most of these references are legitimate enough; many of them are actually concerned with the interpretation of Barth. However, at two points—both on the central issue of Christology—van Buren does invoke the support of Bonhoeffer for his own position:

> If we would define Jesus by his freedom, however, we must emphasize its positive character. He was free from all anxiety and the need to establish his own identity, but he was above all free for his neighbor. This was the characteristic which Bonhoeffer, in his last writings, found so impressive.[8]

And again, he appeals to the "Outline for a Book" from the *Letters* (the famous passage about "being for others") for the statement:

> We would emphasize, along with many contemporary interpretations of Christology, that the Christian perspective sets the "true nature" of man precisely in the freedom for others which was Jesus' own. *Human* being is being free for one's neighbor.[9]

Now it is a very real question whether Professor van Buren, like Bishop Robinson, has not unwittingly extracted the Bonhoeffer designation "the Man for Others" from its proper theological context and set it down in the context of an Anglo-Saxon liberal ethical humanitarianism. Certainly, there is something highly Pelagian about both the Robinson and the van Buren Christologies. Jesus for both of them is the one man who truly achieved openness for

[7] Van Buren, *The Secular Meaning of the Gospel* (New York: Macmillan, 1963), p. 171.
[8] *Ibid.,* p. 123.
[9] *Ibid.,* p. 163, footnote.

others. He alone really "made it" and thus became a disclosure of the Ground of being (Robinson), of authentic human being (van Buren). Again we are not concerned here to criticize these Christologies as such, but only to press the question whether this is what Bonhoeffer really meant when he spoke of Christ as "the Man for Others."

Of course all this raises the riddle of Bonhoeffer, a riddle which besets any interpreter of the last writings. Are these to be interpreted as new, radical departures, or as natural developments of his earlier theology? Is there a radical discontinuity between the earlier and the later writings, or can we discern hints and suggestions of his latest thoughts even in such early works as *Communion of Saints* and *Act and Being?*

In Germany the riddle of Bonhoeffer has characteristically produced two schools of interpretation. On the one hand, there are those who focus on the ecclesiological and christological aspects of Bonhoeffer's writings, and who are therefore led to emphasize the continuity to be found throughout them. On the other hand, there are those who focus on the hermeneutical implications of the *Letters.* This second school is represented in Gerhard Ebeling's essay "On the Non-religious Interpretation of Biblical Concepts" which has appeared in English translation.[10]

The chief representatives of the ecclesiological-christological school of Bonhoeffer interpretation are Ernst Wolf and Jürgen Moltmann.[11]

The essays translated for the present volume should serve to acquaint the English-speaking world more fully with the ecclesiological-christological school of Bonhoeffer interpretation in Germany.

[10] In *Word and Faith* (1963), pp. 98–161. Further examples from this school of interpretation will be found in the recently published volume *World Come of Age,* ed. R. Gregor Smith (Philadelphia, 1967). See especially the essay by Hanfried Müller (*op. cit.,* pp. 182–214). Müller, a professor at the Humboldt University in (East) Berlin, provides an interesting analogy to Robinson and van Buren. Whereas the latter have transposed Bonhoeffer into an Anglo-Saxon context of liberal ethical humanitarianism, Müller develops Bonhoeffer's ethical and social thought along Marxist lines.

[11] Cf. also the essay by the Danish systematic theologian Regin Prenter in *World Come of Age,* pp. 93–130. While this essay is mainly concerned with Bonhoeffer's gravamen against Barth for his positivist doctrine of revelation, it also exhibits an incidental concern for the continuity between the earlier and the later Bonhoeffer. See especially *op. cit.,* p. 129.

The first essay is by Jürgen Moltmann. It demonstrates very clearly that Bonhoeffer's Christology and especially his concept of "the Man for Others" is rooted in the Pauline doctrine of the second Adam and the principle of "vicarious representation" (*Stellvertretung*). How pertinent this is to the English-speaking world, how relevant in view of the use to which the seminal thoughts of the *Letters* have been put by our radical theologians, will be immediately apparent from the following passage:

> In *Ethics* and in his last letters from . . . Tegel, Bonhoeffer could call this vicarious action "Being for others" (Christ the man who lives for others). This has been widely misunderstood in a moralistic sense as general humanitarian love. But here (sc. in *Communion of Saints*), where the idea first occurs in his earliest writings, its strictly christological basis is obvious. Vicarious representation is not a moral possibility or norm (p. 44).

Another quotation will demonstrate the christological basis of the concept of worldly holiness:

> For Bonhoeffer the dominion of Christ and "authentic worldliness" become interchangeable terms once they are seen in the light of deputyship (*Stellvertretung*). Take also his positive understanding of the "world coming of age" and the "completely worldly life" in the last letters. This means in the final analysis only that the world has become world and man human as a result of their christocratic liberation from heteronomy and autonomy (pp. 65 f.).

From these quotations we can see how the characteristic key words upon which our Anglo-American radical theologians have pounced, and which they have treated as natural, universal truths, were for Bonhoeffer strictly dependent upon the work of Jesus Christ, upon his incarnation, crucifixion, and ascension. This is because they rise out of the Christology which Bonhoeffer had worked out in his earlier writings.

Jürgen Weissbach is a young scholar, not yet widely known, whose concern with and interpretation of Bonhoeffer are closely parallel to Moltmann's. For this reason it seemed advisable to translate and publish the two essays together. Weissbach's essay indeed is in constant dialogue with Moltmann's earlier article. One might ask whether Weissbach really adds anything to Moltmann. Our answer would be that it brings out the centrality of Bonhoeffer's ethical concern, while at the same time exhibiting its christological foundation and its inner connection with his thinking about Christ and world.

It may be hoped that the publication of these two essays will not only acquaint the English-speaking world more fully with one side of the German debate but will also serve as a warning against the danger of detaching Bonhoeffer's *Ethics* and *Letters and Papers from Prison* from their proper theological context and then reinterpreting their daring ideas in a context which is wholly alien to his thinking.

Jürgen Moltmann

THE LORDSHIP
OF CHRIST
AND HUMAN
SOCIETY

Preface

This essay on the social ethics of Dietrich Bonhoeffer is the outcome of the colloquium on theology and law which has met from time to time since 1949 under the auspices of the Evangelical Church in Germany.[1] These discussions have raised a series of problems. What is the theological basis of law and for theological pronouncements on such institutions as law, marriage, and the state? These problems define and limit the questions with which we shall approach the work of Dietrich Bonhoeffer.

The present study is an expansion of a lecture entitled "Mandate and Institution," delivered July 17, 1958, to the Evangelische Forschungsakademie in the Christopherus-Stift, Heidelberg. While I was preparing this lecture, and as a result of the discussions which followed it, I became interested in the idea of presenting Bonhoeffer's doctrine of the mandates not only in the light of its dogmatic foundations in *Ethics* but also in the context of his theology and social ethics as a whole. Current interpretation of Bonhoeffer suffers from the fact that single ideas from *Ethics* and *Letters and Papers from Prison* are being discussed in isolation. Their original rootage in his earlier systematic writings on the sociology of the church (*Communion of Saints*, written in 1927, published in 1930, and reprinted in 1954) and on theological ontology (*Act and Being*, 1931, 1956) have not received sufficient attention.

---

[1] Cf. the publications *Kirche und Recht* (1950); *Recht und Institution, Glaube und Forschung* 9 (1965); see also the literature resulting from the conversations at Göttingen (1949), Treysa (1950), and Hemer (1955, 1956); and the report entitled "Das Göttinger Rechtsgespräch 1949 und seine Auswirkungen" by E. Wolf in *Recht und Institution*, pp. 9 ff.

We must therefore try to point up certain basic ideas which led to Bonhoeffer's doctrine of the mandates, ideas like "reality" ("deputyship"), "personality," and "sociality." We must attempt to show how Bonhoeffer got at them and how he modified them in his later works. Nor should we forget the contemporary controversies which form the background of his writings, though the writings themselves contain very little that is directly polemical in character. Finally, in discussing Bonhoeffer's *Ethics* we should not forget Luther's social ethics, to which Bonhoeffer gives a new interpretation and application and which, as recent Swedish studies by G. Törnvall and G. Wingren and German studies by E. Wolf and J. Heckel have shown, open up fresh insights. To these we would add some detailed reference to Bonhoeffer's affinity to and difference from Karl Barth, with whom he is in constant dialogue in matters of ethics and ecclesiology. Only in this overall context do the contours of Bonhoeffer's thought stand out clearly, making it possible for us to understand it properly and to carry it to fruitful conclusions.

A comparison of Bonhoeffer's doctrine of the mandates with the outcome of the conferences on institutionalism just mentioned would seem to be promising in two different ways.

First, the doctrine of the mandates has provided a new term unencumbered by previous associations—for Protestantism at any rate—for the discussion and understanding of the institutional phenomena in law, marriage, and the state. This term, "institution," helps us to avoid those *a priori* theological assumptions which would have been inevitable had we adhered to terms like "order" or "estate," "law" or "value." "Institution" points first and foremost toward the divine foundation of these relationships. This opens the way for theology, jurisprudence, and sociology to rediscover one another and engage in a promising dialogue.

Second, in the discussion thus far many have commented, and always favorably, on Bonhoeffer's new insights on such matters as law and mandate, act and being, relation and analogy.[2] But there has never been any study of Bonhoeffer's social ethics as a whole, nor of such central concepts as "deputyship" or "reality," nor of his bold attempt to enumerate and coordinate the mandates. As a

[2] E.g., Ernst Wolf, in *Recht und Institution*, pp. 26 ff.

consequence his suggestions and conclusions have never been tested with a view to their applicability.

By "social ethics" we do not mean "that complete ethical aporia" (*E*, p. 58) resulting from the divorce of the individual from society as opposed to individual ethics. Rather, we mean the descriptive as well as the normative science of human structures and intentions.[3] In making this attempt we fully realize that Bonhoeffer has left us only fragments and perspectives for a social ethic, only visions of the problems involved and pointers for further theological research, not a complete theological system hammered out in controversy.

In conclusion we would remind the reader that this is meant to be no merely academic study of Dietrich Bonhoeffer. We hope to widen the circle of those who pay serious attention to what he has to say and let him play his part in the dialogue which is going on today.

I.

Bonhoeffer's Early Thought

1. SOCIOLOGY AND THE CHURCH

For a long time a discussion has been going on about the sociology of the church, particularly. Bonhoeffer entered into the discussion with a dogmatic examination of the subject in his book *Communion of Saints* ([4]1930; Eng. trans., [1]1960). The language of his work is somewhat dated because of its idealistic frame of reference. But it still represents an impressively high level of scholarship.[1] The discovery of the social intention behind

---

[3] Cf. the definition given by E. Wolf, *Peregrinatio* (Munich: C. Kaiser, 1954), p. 214.

[1] Karl Barth, *Church Dogmatics*, IV/2 (1958), p. 641.

all the basic terms of dogmatics leads Bonhoeffer to a new sociological development of the doctrine of the church. "The concept of the Church is possible only in the sphere of reality based on God; that is, it is not deducible. The reality of the church is a revelation, part of whose nature it is to be either believed or denied" (CS, p. 88). The church of Christ never reveals her essential nature to general observation, whether of sociology or religious sociology. The essential nature of the church can be fully comprehended only from within. Nevertheless, any ecclesiology must draw out the implications of the real nature of the church as revealed to her by Christ in terms of a social philosophy and sociological structures. Only so can the categories of sociology be made meaningful for theology.

What led Bonhoeffer to choose as his subject the sociology of the church? It was the work of the Berlin School, whose founder was Ernst Troeltsch, and particularly Troeltsch's book *The Social Teaching of the Christian Churches*.[2] In the Berlin School the history of the Christian communities and of their ideas of community are treated from an independent historical and sociological perspective. But as Bonhoeffer saw it the real need was to get away from this sociological and historical relativism and to declare war on this kind of theology with its pragmatic sociology. It is impossible to ascertain the proper and essential structure of the church from a merely historical examination of it as an empirical social institution. Bonhoeffer approaches it from the other end: "The inquiry into Christian social philosophy is a genuinely dogmatic one . . . since it can be answered only if our starting point is the concept of the church. . . . The fact that every genuinely theological concept can be correctly comprehended only when set within and supplemented by its special social sphere is proof of the specifically theological nature of any inquiry into the sociology of the church" (CS, Preface). If this method is successful in exposing the "proper social sphere" of Christian, i.e. dogmatic, terms such as "primordial state," "sin," "deputyship," and "community" and in demonstrating the relevance of these dogmas for the doctrine of the church, then the essential sociological structures of the church, which underlie the empirical form of Christian community,

---

[2] New York: Macmillan, [3]1950 = German, 1911.

emerge. "It is in the necessary bond between the basic relation-ships and the empirical form of community as a special form that the nature of the church, formally speaking, resides" (*CS*, p. 87). Thus there is a historicizing as well as a religious misconception of the church, and both must be avoided. The "revelational reality" of the church of Christ cannot be comprehended ade-quately as a historical phenomenon of social history. The church cannot be comprehended historically, but only in its foundation in the reality of God and his revelation. The religious misunder-standing, on the other hand, would be the identification of the church with the eschatological kingdom of God. When that happens, the limitations of man in history are ignored. Either the historical form is objectified and idolized, as in the hierarchical theocracy of the Roman Catholic Church, or it is dismissed as an accident of history, governed by the law of death and sin and without any social relevance. Both the historical and the religious-eschatological approaches misunderstand the reality of the church, which is at once a historical community and a divine institution. Both misunderstand the problem which lies in the simultaneous use of phenomenology and theology to comprehend a reality that is at once historical and eschatological, human and divine.

The problem arising here in the sphere of ecclesiology comes up again in a similar way in connection with the "institutions" or "mandates." "In the first place, these institutions cannot be understood from within, from an analysis of their phenomenal structures. They can only be understood in the light of faith—in the creative word of God which gives them concrete shape. Secondly, and *per contra*, they can never be deduced or under-stood from some abstract, theoretical principle. They can only be understood by constant reference to their concrete historicity within the sphere of phenomenal reality. The ontic, phenomenal peculiarity of the institutions needs ontological and theological illumination because its being is based on the fact that it is grounded in the word of God and united with it." [3]

Bonhoeffer is aware of this coincidence in the "essential struc-ture" of the church. On the one hand, it originates in her em-

[3] Ernst Wolf, in *Recht und Institution*, p. 71.

pirical social acts and, on the other, has to be deduced from "revelational realities." Consequently, his aim is to apply social philosophy, with its basic insights into social concepts and relationships, in the service of Christian dogmatics. Hence, after an introductory section defining his terms, his chapter on social philosophy "investigates the ultimate social relations which are prior to all knowledge of and will for empirical community, and the 'origins' of sociality in man's spiritual life and its essential connection with it. It is the science of the original and essential nature of sociality" (CS, p. 19). But if all dogmatic definitions have a "social intention," then Bonhoeffer's adoption of the categories of social philosophy must have a polemical purpose as well. Only when transformed and reminted can terms derived from social philosophy, such as "person" and "community," be used for a dogmatic analysis of the sociology of the church.

Bonhoeffer thus shows at the very beginning the direction he intends to take in social philosophy, mainly the social philosophy of German idealism. And it is a direction which he is to follow until he reaches the social ethics of the "mandates." By this we do not simply mean the use of a particular terminology derived from idealism. This increasingly disappears from the later writings. By addressing himself to the socio-philosophical question of the "origins" and the "essential structures" of society, Bonhoeffer ceases to reflect on the historical process of the rise and decay of the institutions and the historical ebb and flow of the social process. This is what gives his sociology of the church and, later on, the doctrine of the mandates their peculiar static quality. Sometimes this has been criticized on the ground that it threatens to foreshorten his eschatology and to petrify the dynamics of history in a legalistic way. H. C. von Hase is afraid that "the mystery of the church under the cross before the Last Day is being unveiled in systematic or even in sociological terms." [4] Karl Barth thinks that dropping the whole idea of the mandates would be better "than rushing on to the rigid assertion of human relationships arranged in a definite order." [5]

It is Bonhoeffer's intention to extricate the sociology of the

---

[4] *EvTh*, 4/5 (1955), pp. 171 ff.
[5] *Church Dogmatics* III/4 (1961), p. 22.

church from the historical relativism which can see only the active side of this community, its ebb and flow, but not its true nature in the law and promise of God that alone make possible and determine the history of the church in obedience and disobedience. "This provides theological justification for our sociological method of asking for the essential structure of the church, and not giving an outline of its development from the point of view of the philosophy of history. In principle the course of church history does not teach us any more about its eschatological significance than does the understanding of every present moment" (*CS*, p. 199). So says Bonhoeffer, immediately after quoting Ranke's saying that "every age is in direct relationship with God." What does he mean here by "structure"? Bonhoeffer himself insists that we should distinguish between "structure and intention" (*CS*, p. 213). "The structure of the whole is visible only in the intention of individual acts, but it is in principle independent of them." This is how he seeks to differentiate a purely ontological social concept from an empirical one. By "essential structure" is implied something like a given basic pattern, realized in the act of acceptance but not identical with the act; still less, created by it.[6]

When Bonhoeffer speaks of the essential structure of the church of Christ he does not have in mind any particular form of the church in history, and certainly not "Christ himself made an object of sociological comprehension."[7] When he speaks in *Ethics* of the "structures of responsible life" he does not refer to rigid human relationships. What he means is the unalterable essential structures that are visible in empirical acts but are not changed by them or, as he later says in the same work: "The will of God therefore is not an idea, still demanding to become real; it is itself a reality already in the self-revelation of God in Jesus Christ. Nor is the will of God simply identical with what is in being, which would mean that it would be fulfilled by submissive acquiescence in things as they are. It is on the contrary a reality whose purpose is to become real ever anew in what is in being and against what is in being" (*E*, p. 77). This still leaves unanswered certain questions. Can the divine foundation in promise

[6] Cf. the ensuing discussion of *Act and Being*.
[7] H. C. von Hase, *EvTh*, 4/5 (1955), p. 171.

and law be equated with the "essence" of the church, with all the metaphysical implications that that involves? Can the will of God be regarded as "reality urging realization in what is in being and against what is in being"? In both of these translations lurks the Platonic doctrine of Ideas.[8] Bonhoeffer himself later opposed this confusion between ontological and kerygmatic statements, castigating it as "the essence of fanaticism": "The direct testimony of the Scriptures is frequently confounded with ontological propositions. This error is the essence of fanaticism in all its forms. For example, if we take the statement that Christ is risen, and present it as an ontological proposition, it inevitably dissolves the unity of the Scriptures, for it leads us to speak of a mode of Christ's presence which is different from e.g. that of the synoptic Jesus. The truth that Jesus is risen and present to us is then taken as an independent statement with an ontological significance which can be applied critically to other ontological statements and it is thus exalted into a theological principle. The assertion that Christ is risen and present is, when taken strictly as a testimony given in the Scriptures, true only as a word of the Scriptures. This word is the object of our faith. There is no other conceivable way of approach to this truth except through this word" (CD, p. 206, n. 1). In view of the distinction Bonhoeffer draws here between ontological and kerygmatic statements, we are tempted to ask how far it is possible to construct a sociology of the church in terms borrowed from social philosophy. How far can we get in expressing the "social intention" of dogmatic concepts in sociological categories? Is it possible to combine in a single term the "empirical church and the essential church," i.e., the church of faith and promise, not the nature of its historical manifestation? Can we grasp logically and sociologically, and at the same time theologically, the sociological and theological implications of the statement that "the church is grounded in the revelation proceeding from the very heart of God"?[9] Bonhoeffer's use of such words as "structure," "essence," and "reality" can be properly understood only when it is realized that he applies them in a new, kerygmatic sense.

[8] This doctrine is latent in the idealistic terminology employed by Bonhoeffer.
[9] E. Wolf, in Sanctorum Communio, p. 5.

2. ECCLESIOLOGICAL PERSONALISM
AND THE SOCIOLOGICAL TRANSCENDENCE

This adoption and reminting of the vocabulary of social philosophy must now be put to the test in the light of Bonhoeffer's comparison of the Christian concept of the personal and of basic social relations with those of social philosophy. The question is: How were these social relations conceived? What is their relevance for the doctrine of the church? Bonhoeffer first discusses the various metaphysical systems: Aristotle, Stoicism, Democritus, and Epicurus. Then he turns to the concept of personality as seen afresh in the epistemology of Descartes and developed by Kant, thus becoming normative for German idealism in the nineteenth century. It is particularly in his discussion of the epistemological doctrine of personality that Bonhoeffer develops a theological personalism exhibiting undeniable affinities with the personalistic thought emerging in the early twentieth century in such philosophers as Dilthey, Buber, Grisebach, Gogarten, Rosenstock-Huessy, and others, though with a distinctive slant of his own.[10]

The metaphysical scheme does not do justice to the essential nature of personality. It either subsumes personality under a more general category or takes it as a specific instance of a general type. A considerable transformation of the Aristotelian and Thomist metaphysical substance took place in Descartes and Kant, with their epistemological doctrine of personality: the reflective and self-asserting Ego becomes the center of a cosmological understanding, the reality of which is neutralized and materialized into an "object." Connected with this is a "loss of being" [11] manifesting itself in the loss of history, the loss of the primary, personal

---

[10] For contemporary discussion on this subject see E. Schlink, "Weisheit und Torheit," *KuD* I (1955), pp. 1 ff.; G. Gloege, "Der theologische Personalismus als dogmatisches Problem," *KuD* I, pp. 23 ff.; H. Diem, "Dogmatik zwischen Personalismus und Ontologie," *EvTh* 15 (1955), pp. 408 ff. On the history of theological personalism cf. G. Gloege, "Person, Personalismus," in *Evangelisches Kirchenlexikon*, Vol. III (Göttingen: Vandenhoeck und Ruprecht, 1959), cols. 129 ff.

[11] Karl Jaspers, *Descartes und die Philosophie* (²1948), pp. 79 ff.

I-Thou relationship leading in the end to a loss of genuine sociality.

On the development of the mechanistic view of the world and the attempt to get beyond it in modern theoretical physics see G. Howe, *Der Mensch und die Physik* ([3]1958), pages 42 ff. and K. Jaspers on Descartes, *op. cit.*, page 85: "The world has become as it were curdled; it is not the sea of being, but being is turned into a mechanical piece of clockwork."

This is just the point where Bonhoeffer sees the beginning of the development of the Western, godless world come of age: "I began by saying that God is being increasingly edged out of the world, now that it has come of age. Knowledge and life are thought to be perfectly possible without him. Ever since Kant, he has been relegated to the realm beyond experience" (*LPP*, p. 208).

In Kant the development of the epistemological concept of the person has made the perceiving I the starting point for all philosophy. His synthesis of transcendental apperception resolved both the I-Thou relation and the opposition of subject and object in the higher unity of the mind, of intellectual intuition. This meant a fresh attempt in philosophy to master the problem of basic social relations (*CS*, p. 25). The subject-object pattern, so central to German idealism, can never offer a way to any sociological category. Bonhoeffer recalls Fichte, the only idealistic philosopher who felt the inadequacy of idealistic categories as a key to the problem of the "other," and Fichte's questionable conclusion: "The concept of the Thou arises by union of the 'It' and the 'I' " (*CS*, p. 212). The Thou might be recognizable as the "alien I." A synthesis of the spirit-world can then be pictured only in a plurality of atomistic I's and as a unity in a spirit which transcends and elevates it. There is no way here to the concept of community, but only to those of identity and unity.

In order to grasp the social concept of the person, Bonhoeffer starts from the notion of "concrete time." The epistemological understanding of time as a purely intuitive form remains unaffected when he says: "At the moment when he is addressed the person is responsible, or, in other words, faced with a decision. This person is not the idealist's reasoning person or personified mind but a particular, living person" (*CS*, p. 30). Thus, from this concept of time, follows a conclusion which is meaningless for the idealist: "The person is continually arising and passing the time. It is not something timelessly existing, it has a dynamic and not a static character; it exists only when a man is morally responsible; it is continually recreated in the perpetual change inherent in all life" (CS, pp. 30 f.). Idealism has no conception of movement or history, no understanding of the moment. "It is a Christian recognition that the person, as a conscious person, is created at the moment when a man is moved, when he is faced with responsibility, when he is passionately involved in moral struggle, and confronted by a claim that overwhelms him. Concrete personal being arises from the concrete situation" (CS, p. 31). Personality thus stands in a genetic connection with the concrete moment of encounter and decision. This concrete situation of encounter does not mean just a casual meeting, but the event of the "ethical barrier." It means ethical, not epistemological, transcendence. "The human person comes into being only in relation to the divine person which transcends it, opposing and subjugating it" (CS, p. 31). The Christian person arises solely from the absolute distinction between God and man; only from the experience of the barrier does the self-knowledge of the moral person arise. The transcendence of the Thou has nothing to do with epistemological transcendence. It is a purely moral transcendence which is experienced only by the man who makes a decision that can never be demonstrated by anyone outside (CS, p. 33). Thus all that is to be said about the Christian concept of the person can be grasped only by one who himself is involved in responsibility (CS, p. 33). Here we must add in parenthesis that this ethical and sociological doctrine of transcendence was always central to Bonhoeffer right down to his last letters (LPP, [1]1953, [2]1962).

Bonhoeffer's protest against the religious misunderstanding of Christianity is, in its theological and philosophical roots, a protest against the confusion between the epistemological experience of transcendence, and ethical and sociological transcendence: "Transcendence consists not in tasks beyond our scope and power but in the nearest Thou to hand" (LPP, p. 238, corrected). "The 'beyond' of God is not the beyond of our perceptive faculties. Epistemological transcendence has nothing to do with the tran-

scendence of God. God is the 'beyond' in the midst of our life"
(*LPP*, p. 166, slightly revised).

As I see it, Bonhoeffer's last visions of the "profound this-sidedness of Christianity" and of "a world come of age" can be fully
understood only when viewed againgst the background of his
early personalism and of the doctrine of sociological transcendence
in the I-Thou relationship developed here. We encounter the
Thou of God in the concrete Thou of social life. Men become
the likeness of God through their impact of their fellow men, and
that in two different ways.

First, as the created Thou. The divine Thou first creates the
human Thou, and because the latter has been willed and created
by God it is a real, holy, and absolute Thou like the divine Thou.
The I-Thou relationship is not a floating relationship. "No man
can of himself make the other into an I, into a moral person conscious of responsibility. God, or the Holy Spirit, comes to the concrete Thou; only by his action does the other become a Thou for
me, from which my I arises. In other words, every human Thou is
an image of the divine Thou" (*CS*, p. 36). Just as the quest for the
essence of the human person becomes the quest for the origin of
the person and can be answered only from the event of the historic call by God, so, too, the quest for the divine image turns its
back on the quest of the quintessence of man as such to his
relationship for the other, and can be answered only from the
event of the I-Thou relationship.

Luther makes the same point: "His statements regarding the
image of God in man do not denote qualities possessed by man.
They are 'merely reflexes of designations for God's action' (Link).
Man in relation to God is not subject but object. Man's being
thus can only be described as God's history with him." [12]

The question is not what man is in himself but, rather, what
he is in the event of the encounter with and for the other. "The
Christian person—though not only the Christian person—consists
in this continual coming into being" (*CS*, p. 37). It stands in a
genetic connection with its relation to others.

Second, men become a pattern for each other, a "larva" or an
instrument of the divine claim. This claim is not that of a created
Thou in general, but as the created "incarnate Thou" of God in

[12] G. Gloege, *KuD* I, p. 26.

a concrete situation. "Since I first know God's 'I' in the revelation of his love, so too, with the other man: here the concept of the church finds its place. Then it will become clear that the Christian person achieves his true nature when God does not confront him as Thou, but 'enters into' him as I" (CS, p. 37). This means that Bonhoeffer does not deduce the claim in the neighbor only from creation and from the "larvae" God wears in history, but from the incarnation of God in Christ. It is only "God entering into man"—here is the christological concept that is so central right down to *Ethics*—that makes concrete a man's "becoming Christ for another" (Luther), the likeness of the living God in intercession, self-oblation, and forgiveness of sins. Only here, in the community of Christ, in the church, does he see the other no longer as claim but essentially as a gift, no longer as law but as gospel (CS, p. 119).

The high point of Bonhoeffer's personalism is to be found in the community of Christ, in the church. Here is a shrewd criticism of the existential personalism of Kierkegaard. Bonhoeffer is aware of his own affinity to Kierkegaard in his opposition to idealism over the concrete reality of the person. "Kierkegaard's ethical person exists only in the concrete situation, but it has no necessary connection with a concrete Thou. The I itself establishes the Thou; it is not established by it" (CS, p. 212). Thus in the last resort Kierkegaard remained faithful to the idealist position, and so he founded an extreme individualism which can attribute only a relative significance to the other. It is of interest that the same criticism is found in Martin Buber.[13]

In presenting the category of the individual, Kierkegaard remarks: "Everyone should exercise the greatest caution in dealing with the other. Essentially, he should talk only with God and with himself." That is a subtle misunderstanding of God. As Buber says: "Creation is no hurdle on the way to God, it is the way itself. Creatures are put in my way so that through them and with them I, their fellow creature, may find my way to God. A God who could be found without them would not be the God of all being, in whom all being finds its fulfillment." [14] As Buber also says a little later in the same work: "When Luther got mar-

[13] Buber, *Dialogisches Leben* (Zürich: Gregor Müller Verlag, 1947), pp. 204 ff.
[14] *Ibid.*, p. 207.

ried, it was a symbolic action. He wanted to extricate the believer of his day from a fossilized religious withdrawal which in the last resort withdrew him from grace, and to open up for him a life with God in the world. But Kierkegaard broke off his engagement because he wanted to lead the unbeliever of his day to become an individual, to a solitary life of faith, to a life alone with God." And in this connection Buber [15] quotes a lovely hasidic story: "The story is told that a man, filled with zeal for God, once left this created sphere and entered into the great vacuum. There he wandered until he came to the gates of the mystery. He knocked. A voice came from within, 'What wouldst thou here?' 'I have,' he replied, 'proclaimed thy praise in the ears of mortals, but they were deaf to me. So I came to thee to be received and rewarded by thee.' 'Then turn thee round,' came the voice from within, 'there is no ear for thee here. Into the deafness of the mortals I have sunk my hearing." [16]

Buber detects in Kierkegaard a hidden Marcionism devoid of any logical basis. The very concept of the divine image as a created endowment of the human Thou makes Kierkegaard's personalism an idea which misses the truth about God and man. How much more forcefully does Bonhoeffer's distinctive conception of the incarnation as the entry of God in human reality expose this weakness in Kierkegaard's category of the individual. It is a category which inevitably misses the truth about the community of Christ in the church.

There is also a second point of criticism. As will be seen from the above discussion, Bonhoeffer goes a long way with Gogarten in his personalism, which is one of principle. But Bonhoeffer parts company with Gogarten at a crucial point—namely, the point at which Bonhoeffer starts thinking in christological and ecclesiological terms. For Gogarten, the contrast between God's word and man's listening is constitutive. The word effectualized in law and gospel qualifies human existence in the given moment. But it does so in such a way that man's historical existence is understood in terms of the law, theologically interpreted. God's demand encounters man under the "larva" of the other. Sometimes the

[15] *Ibid.*, p. 152.
[16] For Buber's criticism of Gogarten's *Politische Ethik* see *Dialogisches Leben*, pp. 244 f.

"larva" takes the form of earthly dominion; sometimes it demands the autonomy of absolute freedom.[17] The word of God, on the other hand, addressing man and making him a person, occurs through the man Jesus of Nazareth. The church, deriving its function from Jesus, "represents" the genuine personality of man, grounded as it is from thence in the pure actuality of the salvation event. That is why the church must be an "absolutely unworldly entity"; not an "organization" but, rather, the "eschatological event of revelation located in the world." Here Bonhoeffer parts company with Gogarten, both on his doctrine of church and later on the question of political ethics. The christological grounding of humanness and human relations in Bonhoeffer's earlier writings is applied to the church as community in Christ. Later, in *Ethics*, it refers to the "larvae" of God that we meet in the world. It is obvious how close Bonhoeffer is to Karl Barth's christological interpretation of man's relations to his fellow men.

Bonhoeffer criticizes Barth's exposition in the *Epistle to the Romans* on the same ground as he criticizes Kierkegaard: "What authority has Barth for saying that the other 'in himself' is trivial and temporal (*Epistle to the Romans*, Eng. trans., p. 452), when this is the very man that God commands us to love? God has made our neighbour 'of supreme significance' in himself. The other man is not only 'a parable of the wholly other . . . the emissary' of the unknown God; but he is of supreme significance in himself, because God considers him significant. Am I ultimately to be in the world alone with God? . . . The second difference between Barth and ourselves is in our conception of *communio*. 'To be one' with God and with one's neighbour is not something which I do for God; . . . the neighbour is not a sort of tool by means of which I practise the love of God. 'To be one' with God and with one's neighbour is something totally different from having communion with him. Barth however makes the two things synonymous" (*CS*, p. 227).

In *Church Dogmatics* III/2 (pp. 203 ff.) this position is revised by Barth in the context of the doctrine of creation. Barth here criticizes Nietzsche's exposure of solitary humanity, frequently echoing Bonhoeffer's personalism.

[17] Cf. the brief presentation by G. Gloege, *KuD* I, pp. 29 ff.

3. THE SOCIOLOGY OF PERSONAL COMMUNITY

"Man's entire spirituality is interwoven with sociality, and rests upon the basic relation of I and Thou" (CS, p. 48). If the primary constitution of personality is its social relation, the result is that human language, human thought, and human purposes are originally at home only in a social setting and can be thought of only in this relation. Only in the reciprocal effect of I and Thou do language, thought, and purpose arise. "With language a system of social spirituality is set within man; in other words, 'objective spirit' has become effective in history" (CS, p. 46), says Bonhoeffer, quoting in support Edmund Husserl, Hans Freyer, and Martin Buber. Similarly, self-consciousness emerges simultaneously with the consciousness of standing in community. "The I and the Thou are fitted into one another in infinite nearness, in mutual penetration, for ever inseparable, resting on one another, in inmost mutual participation, feeling and experiencing together, and sustaining the general stream of spiritual interaction. Here the openness of personal being is evident" (CS, p. 48). But this sociality implies an equilibrium between personal and social being, each conditioning the other. As personality is born from social being, so in turn it gives birth to the personal being of sociality. The characteristic form in which the stream of encircling spirituality is experienced and in its turn first takes shape in history is the form of the Thou. This argues against Hegel's principle of spirit. Personal spirit in its individual manifestation lives only in virtue of sociality. Yet, on the other hand, the "social spirit" comes into being only in individual form. This authentic sociality is impelled toward personal unity, but so far from suppressing or annihilating that unity, it actually constitutes it and brings it to life. There is no question of priority, but only of reciprocal relationship.

Just as Hegel's idealism threatens to belittle personal individuality, so modern existentialism is in danger of misunderstanding the destructive character, inaugurated by Kierkegaard and Heidegger, of sociality—or worse, in danger of preventing its achievement. Is social unity, then, exhausted in the changes of personal interaction? "In theological language, does God mean by community something that absorbs individual man, or is God solely concerned with the individual? (*CS*, p. 50). The "equilibrium" postulated forbids a onesided calculation of this interaction; also —and this term of Bonhoeffer's appears particularly relevant today—it rules out any existential reduction of the individual to a state of monologue in which he escapes from his bondage to "*das 'Man'* " and discovers his authenticity only by himself. The principle of the equilibrium between personal and social being makes it imperative to reflect further on the structures of community. The social being of the community is not exhaustively defined by the number of individuals comprising it and their interaction with one another but represents something new and supra-personal. Bonhoeffer's terminology here is uncertain, tentative and exploratory. He speaks of "collective personality," in which the individual participates, which transcends the individual, but which is incomprehensible without the correlate of individual personal being (*CS*, p. 51). He speaks of Leibniz's doctrine of the monad (*CS*, p. 52) as a help to understanding the new center of action, which community produces; and of the "community of will" (*CS*, p. 52), as Seeberg calls it; or the "objective spirit" in Hegelian terms. The "net of sociality" is prior to the will to community. The very real relationships it implies are present even where they are totally and consciously rejected. Bonhoeffer does not consider it one of the successful achievements of modern thought that it has emancipated itself from hypostasization of community. Although the vocabulary he uses in working on the problems of the community are only crutches borrowed from the social philosophy of German idealism, which make it impossible to clarify the equilibrium of personal being adequately, yet his vision of the problem is accurate and in its application to the doctrine of the church highly fruitful.[18]

"God created man and woman, each dependent on the other. God does not desire a history of individual men, but the history

---

[18] Cf. today, e.g., Bultmann's reduction of history to individual encounters and decisions in *The Presence of Eternity* (The Gifford Lectures, 1955), (New York: Harper & Row, 1959), pp. 2 ff., 123 ff., and the cautious criticisms of E. Käsemann in *ZThK* 54 (1957), pp. 14 ff.

of the community of men. Nor does he desire a community which absorbs the individual into itself, but a community of men. In his sight the community and the individual are present at the same moment, and rest in one another. The structures of the individual and the collective unit are the same. Upon these basic relations rests the concept of the religious community and the church" (CS, p. 52). It is precisely the doctrine of the church that demands a doctrine of community in which the social being is not exhausted in the I-Thou relationships of individuals. Only after the peculiar and distinctive being of "collective personality" is accounted for can social relations be understood in their full wealth of meaning and in their whole vitality.

As for Bonhoeffer's discussion of the "created" structures of personal and social life, his working assumption has still to be noted. Unlike idealism, it is not a matter of eternal, unchanging, and nonhistorical being, but of theological statements deriving from the doctrine of the primal state and eschatology. This means that both concepts have to be understood historically—the concept of the Christian person and also the concept of an unbroken social community. The reality of sin which infinitely changes human nature "is given concrete expression in the eschatological expectation of the new humanity. The unbroken doctrine of the person must be understood in the light of the notion of the new humanity, which in hope overcomes the history of sin and death" (Sanctorum Communio [German ed.], p. 36). "Thus the problems posed by social philosophy and sociology can only be dealt with in the context of theology, and not in general terms, as befitting the created order. They are presuppositions of revelation and part of its data" (CS, p. 38).

4. THE COMMUNION OF SINNERS
AND THE COMMUNION OF SAINTS

When he comes to apply his doctrine of community to the sociology of sin and the new life, Bonhoeffer ascribes to it a dominant role. He uses the terms "collective person," "objective spirit," and the like to describe it; but such terms have only a heuristic role and are merely crutches borrowed from philosophy.

a) Sin radically changes the relationship between I and Thou and between I and mankind. It results in an "ethical atomism," as Bonhoeffer characterizes the life of the community of sinners: "With sin ethical atomism enters into history. This is essentially applicable to the spiritual form. All the natural forms of community remain, but are corrupt in their innermost core" (*CS*, p. 72). Conscience isolates the sinner in his loneliness before God. This is accompanied by the further perception which does not destroy but rather deepens the first, viz., that the distress of sin is of infinite proportions. "Thus the perception that in sin one is to the highest degree alone leads to the other perception that one's sin is to the widest extent shared" (*CS*, p. 72). From what has been said earlier regarding personality and sociality, sin must be understood as a supra-individual as well as an individual act. " 'The mankind of sin' is one, even though it consists throughout of individuals; it is a collective person and yet subject to endless fragmentation; it is Adam as every individual is both himself and Adam" (*CS*, p. 85). The sinful act, since it is a personal act, is at the same time the act of all mankind in person. The experience of being the chief of sinners and the experience of being in the community of sinners always go hand in hand (Isa. 6).

But how can personal guilt and social involvement in sin be logically combined? How are we to understand "life in Adam" (Rom. 5)? As "original sin" in a metaphysical or biological sense (St. Thomas Aquinas)? As the individual repetition of Adam's sinful act? "Everything clearly depends upon finding the general act in the individual's sinful act, without making the one the basis for the other" (*CS*, p. 79). Bonhoeffer is here applying the results of his social philosophy. He says: The sinful deed of the individual "is at once the deed of the human race, no longer in the biological sense in his person. . . . This relation between the individual and the race also corresponds to the monadic image . . . in which every single monad 'represents' the whole world. . . . Every act is at once an individual act, and one in which mankind's general sin is brought to life again. In this we have established the universality of sin as necessarily given along with and in individual sin" (*CS*, p. 79). In this "given along with," the boundaries of the I have been preserved. But as every I involves a Thou, so too, the whole race is always present in it. Original sin, or as Bonhoeffer prefers it, "universal sin," is only the reverse side, the horizon of personal guilt which accompanies it. Personal guilt for its part is the existential depth of universal sin. The cosmic dimension of guilt is complementary to its existential depth. The one cannot be conceived of without the other. The one cannot be derived from the other. The subject of both is the individual and the race. Sin can be neither moralized nor materialized.

With the above we should compare Bultmann's painstaking exegesis of Romans 5.[19] In discussing the curse that lies upon Adamic mankind, Paul is under the influence of the gnostic myth. But that threatens to make sin a matter of fate, like death itself. Bultmann takes his bearings from Christ, the antitype of Adam, and says: "Through Christ there was brought about no more than the *possibility* of life, which, however, in men of faith becomes certain reality. That suggests, then, that one should assume by analogy that through Adam there was brought about for Adamic mankind the *possibility* of sin and death—a possibility that does not become a reality until individuals become guilty by their own responsible action. Whether that may be regarded as Paul's real thought must, to be sure, remain a question; at any rate the universal fallenness of Adamic mankind to sin and death is beyond all question to Paul." [20] By bringing in the gnostic myth with its inherent determinism, Bultmann blinds himself to the concomitance of individual and universal sin, which Paul affirmed and which Bonhoeffer, in my opinion, rightly saw. The christological antitype does not mean individual redemption but, in Christ, vicarious atonement for the world, and in the church the call to apostolic representation for the world.

The connection between individual and communal guilt is a sociological one. But how can the race, humanity, nation, or the "collective person" be addressed ethically and so be made ethically responsible?

Bonhoeffer points to biblical usage where not only individuals

[19] *Theology of the New Testament* I, trans. Kendrick Grobel (New York: Charles Scribner's Sons, 1952), pp. 251 ff.
[20] *Ibid.*, pp. 252 f.

but also a whole people are addressed by God. And not only single persons but even cities and districts have the gospel preached to them. "It is the Israelite concept of the people of God which arose solely through being thus challenged by God, by the prophets, by the course of political history and by alien peoples. The call is directed to the collective person, and not to the individual. It is the people that is to do penance. . . . The people who must be comforted (Isa. 40:1)" (*CS*, p. 83). God has a purpose for the nation just as he has for the individual. Regarding universal sin, Bonhoeffer can say: "There is not just one sin of the individual German, the individual Christian but also the sin of Germany and the sin of the church." But then he passes in this connection from the "chosen people" without qualification to nations in general and to the German nation in particular. Here he follows Tönnies in conceiving the nation as a mature and eschatological community. He does not take sufficient regard of Israel's election, in which it was specifically and uniquely chosen out of all peoples, but transposes it into nationalistic terms in the way that was popular in the (German) Youth Movement. It is symptomatic of his development that in *Ethics* the nation is not mentioned as one of the divine mandates of God. We cannot discuss here the question of the election of Christian nations, a subject which excites such interest in Dutch theology. But reference should be made to similar tendencies in Bonhoeffer's thought; e.g., when he speaks of "the form of Christ and his taking form in the Christian West" (*E*, pp. 25 ff.), and of "the world come of age in the history of Western secularism" (*LPP*).

"The community which is from God to God, which bears within it an eschatological meaning, this community stands in God's sight and does not dissolve into the fate of the many" (*LPP*). It does not matter whether the whole nation in the sum of its members hears God's call and the complete collective person does penance. That can happen only "within" the individual. Yet it is not the individual but the community which hears in the individual, does penance and believes, insofar as God can see the many in the few (Gen. 18:32), and in One saw all mankind and redeemed it, and insofar as individual penance and faith occur not in private separation from the nation—which is what happens when sin is misinterpreted in an individualistic moralistic way—but "vicariously" for the nation and the whole world. Such an event would, in turn, be commensurate with the sociological interlocking of individual and collective guilt with the depth and breadth of the confession of sin. It is in the total and universal guilt of the individual that universal sin takes concrete shape. Similarly it is in vicarious repentance and intercessory faith that total renewal takes concrete shape. The atomistic solidarity of the communion of sinners is replaced by the representative community, the communion of saints. Or, to put it another way, mankind is a collective person in Adam, and can be replaced only by another collective person, "Christ existing as community."

It is obvious that Bonhoeffer presumes, right up to his last letters, the doctrine of deputyship (which he derived from sociology), the unity of the whole, the "net of sociality," and the "collective person." Although deputyship is a strictly christological doctrine, as will be shown below, it still retains the universal or theocratic structure in which it is grounded. This links Bonhoeffer not only with Hegel, whose concepts he adopted with critical modifications, but also with the Eastern Orthodox idea of community, i.e., *sobornost*. He quotes Khomiakov and Arseniev in important passages in connection with ecclesiology (CS, pp. 235, 132).

b) All of the sociological insights with which Bonhoeffer starts were not originally intended for use only in connection with the communion of saints, though that is where they really become concrete. The relationship of person to person, man to man, the prevolitional form of sociality, the "objective" shape taken by the community spirit—none of all this applies to human nature as such. Rather, it is all relative to the church as a reality grounded in revelation and to the new humanity as an eschatological phenomenon. In terms of social philosophy, the church as "the body of Christ" is, for Bonhoeffer, a collective person. And yet—here he parts with romanticism and idealism—what stands superior to all persons, constituting them and acquiring shape in them, is not universal spirit or the human race, but God's being-for-man in Christ. Only this being of God *pro nobis* is prior to and transcendent over individual persons and their relationships (*extra nos*), and specifically in the mode of deputyship or vicarious representation. In Christ's act of vicarious representation on the cross lies the antecedent ground of the personal and social structure of the church. Vicarious representation between human beings is aroused "intentionally" in the act of love. In Christ all of what is "coming to pass" in the growth and life of the church already "exists." In this same way of vicarious representation the church as the new mankind is already complete in him. This act of God is her being, and it is this being in him that constitutes her history and her growth. Because all mankind is loved, redeemed, and renewed by God in Christ, Christ represents in his life the whole of human history. For "the word of Jesus Christ is the interpretation of His existence, and it is therefore the interpretation of that reality which in history attains to this fulfilment" (*E*, p. 200). In him the whole of Adamite humanity is transformed into the humanity of Christ—vicariously, once and for all. In order, however, that this eschatological fulfillment might happen in time, the will of God is realized ever anew in the power of the Holy Spirit; no longer collectively but in the individual, in the partial community of the church vicariously representing the whole of humanity. This appropriation in act presupposes being in Christ; it is the revelatory act of God in the Holy Spirit. Humanity *is* new in Christ, i.e., from the perspective of eternity; humanity *becomes* new by the action of the Spirit, i.e., seen from the perspective of time. Realization in history does not stand in contrast to making the process possible in Christ. Rather, the reality of the will of God fulfilled in Christ stands in contrast to salvation and being taken up into his vicarious action. Thus, finally, the christological idea of vicarious representation is basic for Bonhoeffer's theology of society. "The vicarious act of Christ contains deep problems of social philosophy" (*CS*, p. 114). This highlights the "social intention" behind all Christian doctrines. Bonhoeffer impregnates all the auxiliary concepts from social philosophy, with which up to then he had been feeling his way, with the idea of deputyship. Bonhoeffer applied sociology to the divine community, the community of the church, and to Christian obedience in responsible action under the mandates of God in the world. Here is the heritage he has left to us, and it is far from being exhausted.

But let us pursue the idea to its source. "In him (i.e., in the vicarious action of Christ) concrete action within time and its being 'for all time' really coincide. There is vicarious action for guilt and punishment. Here the one demands the other, for 'punishment' does not mean to take the consequences of sin upon oneself but to judge these consequences to be a 'punishment' for sin. The idea that the passion of Jesus was in the nature of a punishment has frequently been disputed. Luther laid all possible stress on this. It is conceivable that someone might take the consequences of sin upon himself even in the moral life of society. The unique quality of the Christian idea of acting vicariously is that this action is strictly vicarious with regard to guilt and punishment. . . . But on the felon's cross, vicarious love triumphs; obedience to God triumphs over guilt and thereby guilt is in fact punished and overcome" (CS, p. 113). In *Ethics* and in his last letters from his prison cell at Tegel, Bonhoeffer could call this vicarious action "Being for others" (Christ the man who lives for others). This has been widely misunderstood in a moralistic sense as general humanitarian love. But here, where the idea first occurs in his earliest writings, its strictly christological basis is obvious. Vicarious representation is not a moral possibility or norm. It is nothing else but the reality of the divine love of the church. It is not a moral but a theological principle. Through the Christian principle of vicarious action the new humanity is brought and held together. In it the material particularity of the basic Christian relationship consists (CS, p. 114). So "vicarious action" is, in the last resort, an ontological principle, according to which the new being of man is grounded in justification through Christ. Hence it is not inconsistent with the ethical principle of the individual's full responsibility before God. The vicarious action of Christ is the foundation of responsibility before God and the disclosure of what it means. When Christ occupies the place of man in his despair before God—a despair in which he either longs for authenticity or refuses it—man achieves in him his person before God. Or, as Bonhoeffer puts it: "whereas man acknowledges Christ as acting vicariously for his entire person, he thus owes his entire person to him" (CS, p. 223). Or again, to quote from *Ethics*: "The structure of responsible life is conditioned by two factors; life is bound to man and to God and a man's own life is free. It is the fact that life is bound to man and to God which sets life in the freedom of a man's own life. Without this bond and without this freedom there is no responsibility. Only when it has become selfless in his obligation does a life stand in the freedom of a man's truly own life and action" (*E*, p. 194).

The principle of deputyship, or vicarious action, not only unites the new humanity with Christ but also knits its members together in a new community. "As the love of God through Christ's vicarious action restores communion between God and man, so the human community, too, once again becomes a living reality in love" (*CS*, p. 114).

So, then, the church, as the new humanity established by the vicarious action in Christ, will find itself in a new set of social relationships.

First, the personality of the individual is not absorbed into the corporate entity of the church. The church is not a multiplicity of individuals forming an association without unity. In the vicarious action of the one for the many lies the unity of the many ("Multiplicity of Spirits," *CS*, pp. 117 ff.).

Second, the new humanity finds its focal point in Christ: in him it is justified and sanctified ("Spiritual unity," *CS*, pp. 137 ff.).

Third, this community of God in the vicarious action of Christ becomes effective in the vicarious acts of men for one another, in the sociality of being-for-one-another in the church; in self-sacrifice and love, in intercession and forgiveness of sins ("Community of Spirit," *CS*, p. 118). "Each man sustains the other in active love, intercession and forgiveness of sins through complete vicarious action which is possible only in the church, resting as it does in its entirety upon the principle of vicarious action, that is, upon the love of God. . . . The church and its members are structurally together, and act vicariously for each other, in the strength of the church. This constitutes the specific sociological character of community based on love" (*CS*, p. 136).

Bonhoeffer relates the solitariness of the person before God to the theological interrelationship of the person in community by means of the tension in the two observations of Luther: First, "The challenge of death comes to us all, and no one can die for another. Everyone must fight his own battle with death by himself alone. We can shout in one another's ears, but everyone must be prepared finally to meet death alone. I will not be with you then or you with me." [21] Second, "If I die, I am not alone in death; if I suffer, they suffer with me [sc. Christ] with all holy angels and all the blessed in heaven, and all pious men on earth" (*First Sermon*, p. 13).

The question is: What are the implications of deputyship for the sociology of the church? We would emphasize four points:

First, in Christ's vicarious action for the church we can consider together both act and being; completion in him and realization though the power of the Holy Spirit in new social relationships, of I and Thou and the community: integration and the process of integration, translation into a new situation (or a new being) and the act of acceptance in historic decision and surrender, condition and process.

Second, the vicarious act of God constitutes community and personal being, without dissolving the one in the other.

Third, the idea of vicarious action combines dominion and service, theocracy and cross, into "the dominion of God in condescension and passion" (H. Dombois).

Fourth, the idea of vicarious action combines the church's commission to serve the whole of humanity belonging to God (the church stands vicariously at the place where the whole of humanity should stand before God) and the fulfillment of God's purpose in the church where the new being-in-existence-for-others is dawning in the world. This last implication in the vicarious function of the church in the world is echoed, even in Bonhoeffer's earliest writings, in his fondness for texts like Exodus 32:32 and Romans 9:1 which express a desire for self-sacrifice and vicarious repentance out of love for the people on the part of the prophet or apostle.[22] Thus in the farewell song of Moses we read: "Who

[21] *The First Sermon* (preached at Wittenberg in Lent, 1522), in *WML* II, p. 391.
[22] These are the texts for the mystical and early Lutheran doctrine of *resignatio ad infernum*.

punishes sin and delights in forgiveness, God I have loved this people."

5. THE CONTRIBUTION OF *ACT AND BEING* [23]

In *Act and Being,* Bonhoeffer attempts to develop the suggestions adumbrated in *Communion of Saints.* A discussion of act and being was going on in the circles of dialectical theology at this time. As Bonhoeffer sees it, the dialectical theologians, Barth, Bultmann, and Gogarten, were striving to liberate the divine revelation from all rigid concepts of being, from objectivizing and from manipulable statements and to understand it as pure act. Unfortunately, however, they were bogged down in the transcendentalism of Kant, either in a theocentric way as in Barth, or from an anthropocentric angle as in Bultmann. On the other side were the ontologists. They wanted to make the revelation of God tangible in the form of a dogma, of consciousness, or of the church as an institution. The trouble with them is that they went off at a tangent, trying to ensure men against the incalculable demand of God through a life lived in the realm of objective existence and in a present which he could manipulate.[24]

This analysis of the issues at stake in current theological debate may be open to question—especially when Bonhoeffer lays all the blame at the door of the philosophical systems. But we need not go into all that here. Let us concentrate instead on the way in which Bonhoeffer developed the earlier suggestions he made in connection with the sociology of the church and applied them to "the theological concepts of being" (*AB,* p. 116), which he was then striving to produce.

The church as the mode of being of the divine revelation seems to Bonhoeffer to provide that unity of act and being for which men sought. The church is not a human achievement but a "reality of revelation." As such it is the primary ontological datum

[23] *Act and Being* was first published in 1931, qualifying Bonhoeffer for the post of lecturer in the University of Berlin.
[24] For a parallel movement in the history of jurisprudence, cf. K. Ritter, *Zwischen Naturrecht und Rechtspositivismus* (1956).

in which personal existence and social relations become possible, and so the life of the community of person is constituted in the person and vicarious work of Christ. Here, in the church, God is present in his freedom for mankind, in his promise and his faithfulness to the act of revelation and to the fulfillment of his promise. But he is present not in eternal nonobjectivity (Barth, Bultmann), not in "repeated acts of encounter," but in his faithfulness to his given word (AB, p. 90). By bringing out the biblical testimony to the covenant and faithfulness of God, Bonhoeffer follows the only possible way in which to demolish both theological actualism and theological ontologism.[25] The revelation of God in history is not bound to the moment of existential encounter, not to human limitations and conditions. Bonhoeffer tries to use Luther's Christology as a clue to revelation in act and being: "It is the honour and glory of our God (*unseres Gottes Ehre*), however, that, giving himself for our sake in deepest condescension, he passes into the flesh, the bread, our hearts, mouths, entrails, and suffers also for our sake that he be dishonourably (*unehrlich*) handled, on the altar as on the Cross" (WA 23, p. 157, quoted in AB, p. 81, n. 1). Thus, too, he encounters the formalistic and actualistic understanding of the freedom and contingency of God in revelation: "In revelation it is a question less of God's freedom on the far side from us, i.e., his eternal isolation and aseity, than of his forth-proceeding, his *given* word, his bond in which he has bound himself, of his freedom as it is most strongly attested in his having freely bound himself to historical man, having placed himself at man's disposal. God is not free *of* man but *for* man. Christ is the word of his freedom. God *is there*, which is to say, not in eternal nonobjectivity but (looking ahead for the moment) 'haveable,' graspable in his word within the Church. Here a substantial [understanding] comes to supplant the formal understanding of God's freedom. If it should prove itself, it will suggest a redirection of our attention from revelation seen in terms of the act towards ontological ideas" (AB, pp. 90 f.). It is the faithfulness of God to the bond with which he bound himself to the

---

[25] For a further treatment of this problem, see the essay by O. Weber, "Die Treue Gottes und die Kontinuität der menschlichen Existenz," in *Sonderheft der EvTh* (1952), pp. 131 ff.

covenantal promise that imparts to his revelation in history the characteristics of his own unity. The characteristic of God is not his absoluteness but the "continuity of his freely kept relationship to mortals, the continuity of his chosen love and faithfulness." [26] The argument about act and being in the revelation of God presupposes the ontological concept of God and the epistemological doctrine of transcendence. Only the premise has been changed; only after theology starts by identifying God's nature with his faithfulness and his revelation with his covenant can this antithesis be overcome. Then theology will be transposed into the "sociological category," which is what Bonhoeffer seeks to achieve. God's action is God's being. But this does not mean he is one object among others. His being is "being-for-mankind." God's will is to be the God of man, in unchanging faithfulness.[27]

It is worth noting that Gloege has attempted to combine the complementary truths of ontology and personalism in very much the same way: "Revelation means God's self-determination and self-limitation. Right down to the empirical level God gives himself by offering concrete, disposable tokens (historical Jesus, word, sacrament). Revelation creates in the realm of the empirical a supra-personal 'being in the church.' . . . This is the all-embracing ontological datum where personal existence becomes feasible." To return to Bonhoeffer: what he says in *Act and Being* has crucial implication for the humanity of man. He does not bear the ground of his humanity in himself. His continuity with himself is not demonstrable from within. At the same time he does not stand before God in the dimensionless constriction and loneliness of momentary existence. This faithfulness of God—proleptically, by a kind of predestination, man's existence is always not just momentarily, though always grasped in the concrete moment —affected existence, recreated existence—existence in social relationships, existence in relation to Christ (*AB*, p. 124). His existence is not a static mode of being, nor does it evaporate into nonentity, but by Christ's vicarious action for him it is established as personal and social being in the community. In God's faithfulness to his promise, man is emancipated from the empirical bonds

---

[26] O. Weber, *op. cit.*, p. 137.
[27] G. Gloege, *KuD* I, p. 41.

of his nature, nationality, and culture, and translated into the history of God. He stands in the tradition of Abraham's blessing of Isaac and Jacob; and again in the divine faithfulness to the preaching of the gospel in which God accepts his people from generation to generation. Here he gives himself to his new humanity so that his person embraces all whom he has won, binding itself in duty to them, and them in reciprocal duty to him (AB, p. 121). "If the being of revelation is fixed in entity, it remains past, existentially impotent; if it is volatilised into the non-objective, its continuity is lost. And so the being of revelation must enjoy a mode of being which satisfies both claims, embodying both the continuity proper to being and the existential significance of the act. It is as such a mode of being that we understand the person and the community. . . . Only thus, in the concretion of the mode of being of a true (i.e. Christ-founded) community of persons, can one observe and preserve the hovering between entity and non-entity. . . . Revelation's mode of being, on the other hand, is definable only with reference to persons. . . . In the social context of the person the static ontology of 'there is' is set in motion. There is no God that 'there is.' God 'is' in the personal reference, in (this) being is his being a person" (AB, pp. 124 ff.).

In the old grammatical and ontological thesis of medieval Scholasticism, *operari sequitur esse* ("act follows being"). All movements and relationships must be understood as predicates of being. But now, owing to modern natural science no less than to the widespread renaissance of biblical and Reformation theology, this Aristotelian definition has proved inadequate.[28] The discovery of relativity in physics and the witness of the reality of God which includes nature and attributes, being and action, is obviously not hospitable to this type of ontological thinking.[29] Does being come before action or action before being? In answer to this question, Bonhoeffer proposes a bold interpretation of a quotation from Luther. The passage in question reads as follows:

[28] See G. Howe, "Parallelen zwischen der Theologie Karl Barths und der heutigen Physik," *Antwort* (K. Barth's Festschrift), (Zollikon-Zurich: Evang. Verlag, 1956), pp. 410 ff.
[29] See E. Schlink, *op. cit.*, pp. 1 ff.; K. Barth, *Church Dogmatics* II/1; III/2 (1960).

"For being comes before doing, but being-acted-upon comes before being. Hence becoming, being, acting follow one another" ("Prius enim esse quam operari, prius autem pati quam esse. Ergo fieri, esse operari se sequuntur").[30] There is of course no inherent contradiction between Luther's statement here and Aristotelian logic. The passage may be compared with another, occurring a little later in the same work: "Non-being is something without a name and man in sin; becoming is justification; being is righteousness; acting is to act and live righteously; to be acted upon is to be made perfect and complete. These five are somehow always in motion" ("Non esse est res sine nomine et homo peccatis; fieri est iustificatio; esse est iustitia: opus est iuste agere et vivere; pati est perfici et consummari. Et hec quinque semper velut in motu sunt [in homine]").[31]

To return to the first of the two quotations from Luther's *Lecture on Romans*, Bonhoeffer's interpretation goes far beyond that of the young Luther: "In relation to God man has the passive position, is a sufferer: Luther is speaking of the *nova nativitas*. Existence is defined as *pati*; 'authentically,' that is to say, one can speak of existence only as of existence which undergoes. . . . Existence in this sense is existence in social context" (*AB*, pp. 126 f.). This *pati*, the suffering and the passion, precedes act and being. "Here I, the historically whole man, individual and humanity together, am encountered, affected. I believe; that is I know myself borne: I am borne (*pati*), therefore I am (*esse*), therefore I believe (*agere*). The circle closes. For even *agere* is *pati* here; but the I always remains the historical One—though in faith the New One (*AB*, p. 131). "The being of revelation, as hovering between the objective and the non-objective is 'person'— the revealed person of God and the personal community of which that person is foundation. Here the transcendental thesis of 'being only in the act,' and the original ontological principle of being independent of the act, unexpectedly coalesce. . . . The transcendental and ontological theses here are combined in the sociological category" (*AB*, p. 133).

---

[30] Martin Luther, *Lecture on Romans*, in *LCC* 15 (Philadelphia: The Westminster Press, 1961), p. 321, n.1.
[31] *Lecture on Romans, op. cit.*, p. 322.

Thus Bonhoeffer penetrates the philosophical dialectic of act and being to arrive at the "social category." Hence we can no longer speak of the nature of God as such. The way is opened for a view of God as person in relation to the covenant with men. Protestant orthodoxy still clung to the doctrine of the eternal immutability of God as the only way of maintaining the distinctive character of God conceived in ontological terms. But now it can be translated into sociological terms as the faithfulness of God in history, in a way which does justice to the biblical testimony. God's being is always his being-for-man. In his revelation in Christ the God who is constant in himself is the God who is constant in his faithfulness to the promise he has given. By analogy, it is no longer possible or necessary to raise the question of man's "nature." The way is opened for a view of man as person, of man as the partner to God's covenant or, in Bonhoeffer's own terms, of a man as the new man in Christ, in the church. Thus the idealistic definition of nature and the actualist definition of history are transcended, and man's being is described as "being-in," expressed in sociological terms.

In this context we are carried a step further by Karl Barth's suggestion about special ethics.[32] Barth, like Bonhoeffer, drops altogether the question of the "essential structure" of God and the "essential structure" of man. However, he speaks of the trinitarian being of God as Creator, Reconciler, and Redeemer, and of man's definition, in divine history, as creature, sinner, and child. "In the succession of these three forms man also appears as a particular being." Hence the task of special ethics is to describe this history of God and man from the creation to atonement and redemption. It does not therefore presuppose either a theology in which the nature of God or an anthropology in which the nature of man is defined. Rather, it deals with the encounter between God and man in these three forms as defining the history of man. It is in this history that man appears as a defined being. This is the trinitarian development of Barth's early statements, which were misinterpreted in an actualist sense, and which Bonhoeffer had in view when he criticized Barth. At any rate, it would be quite conceivable to develop Bonhoeffer's suggestion

[32] *Church Dogmatics* III/4 (1961), pp. 21 ff.

about the faithfulness of God in the vicarious action of Christ, in his being-for-man, along trinitarian lines, with God as Creator, Reconciler, and Redeemer. In the same way, too, Bonhoeffer's conception of man's being in the church could be developed in terms of a divine history, in which man appears as creature, sinner, and child. Actually, however, this would seem to be where Bonhoeffer and Barth part company, Bonhoeffer with his theocentric Christology and Barth with his trinitarian Christology.

Bonhoeffer always thought of the incarnation in purely ecclesiological and christological terms. It was the "entrance of God" into man and real human life. There is a kind of static rigidity about Bonhoeffer's doctrine of the incarnation, with slight overtones of modalism, whereas Barth's trinitarian thinking gives a new slant to the doctrine of the incarnation. The traditional doctrine of the incarnation comes to life. The basic categories of ontology-concepts are used to describe a process in a state of flux. The unity of God and man is interpreted as "history," not as a static condition.

6. THE "ANALOGIA RELATIONIS"

It was in *Communion of Saints* that Bonhoeffer first saw and described the I-Thou relationship between man in analogy to the Thou relationship of man to God. It is only in connection with his effect on his neighbor that man can be called the image of God. The Christian person does not achieve his full stature until God ceases to stand aloof as a "Thou" and enters into it as an "I." Only in that fellowship with God in which Christ through the Holy Spirit enters human life does the church become involved with humanity. Only then does the new human fellowship take concrete shape in analogy to man's likeness to God. This idea is developed a step or two further in Bonhoeffer's exposition of Genesis, chapters 1–3.[33] Here, in a discussion of human freedom, he shows what he means by the *analogia relationis*, a term he had coined himself. Man's likeness to the Creator consists in his freedom. But freedom is not something man has for himself or

[33] CF (German ed., ¹1933; Eng. trans., ¹1959).

can find in himself. "Freedom is a relationship and nothing else." [34] It is a relationship between two persons. To be free means "being free for the other" because this other has bound me to him. Only in relationship with the other am I free. No substantial or individualistic concept of freedom can conceive of freedom. I have no control over freedom as over a property. It is simply the event that happens to me through the other (*CF*, p. 35). Consequently the archetype of this freedom in sociality cannot be the absolute freedom of a God-in-himself. The exemplar and sacrament of this freedom for the other is God's freely given grace in which God elects freedom not for himself but for man. Man's freedom for the other, where it occurs, is the result of the event of God's freedom for man in Christ. For it is in him that God creates his image on earth. "Here created *freedom* means—and it is this that goes beyond all previous deeds of God, the unique *par excellence*—that God himself enters his creation. Now God does not only command, and his word come to pass, he himself enters into creation and thus creates freedom" (*CF*, p. 36).

This "image . . . after our [God's] likeness," created by God-made-man, is consequently not an *analogia entis*. It is not the likeness of a lower being to the structure of a higher being in itself—and this because, and only because, of this christological reason. If God cannot be thought of as being for himself but as bearing witness to his "being for man" in Christ, then we can speak only of *analogia relationis*. Thus the analogy lies in the correlation of these relations on which divine and human existence are founded. This means that the relationship is not a structure of human being as such, but a given, set relationship, *iustitia passiva*. Further, man can comprehend this analogy only in view of the divine original. "*Analogia relationis* is therefore the relation given by God himself and is analogy only in this relation given by God. The relation of creature with creature is a God-given relation because it exists in freedom and freedom originates from God" (*CF*, p. 37).

Only in this act of giving, and therefore only in the event of

[34] Cf. also Buber's principle, "In the beginning is relationship" (*Dialogisches Leben*, p. 30).

"cooperation" and the integration of man into the dominion of God in Christ does the *analogia relationis* come to life.

Bonhoeffer does not mean that the divine likeness is given simply in creation as though it were an analogy resulting from the likeness of cause and effect. "The work does not resemble the Creator, it is not his image. It is the form of his command" (*CF*, p. 33). He is obviously not thinking of the resemblance between man and his fellows and between the persons of the Trinity. His whole idea of analogy is based on the real presence of God in Christ, on the "entering of God" into the created order. Karl Barth borrowed the concept of the *analogia relationis* from Bonhoeffer. But he obviously uses it in a different sense and in a trinitarian context.[35]

II.

Theocracy and Christology

The crucial issue in social ethics is not the sociology of the church itself but the application of the resultant theological ontology to phenomena of secular institutions, to the order, classes, estates, or mandates existing alongside and within the church and in partnership with which the church must seek the will of God. In order to gain the right perspective on Bonhoeffer's social ethics of the mandates let us insert here a theological parenthesis on "Theocracy and Christology." In this chapter we will endeavor to grasp the dogmatic outline of *Ethics*. At the same time we hope to lay bare the far-reaching shift in Bonhoeffer's thinking which bore such fruitful consequences later. This shift took place be-

[35] Cf. *Church Dogmatics* III/1 (1958), pp. 184 ff., 196 ff.; III/3, (1960), pp. 49 ff. On the difference between the theological doctrine of relation and the Aristotelian philosophy of substance, cf. E. Schlink, *op. cit.*

tween *The Cost of Discipleship* (written in 1937) and the war-
time writings—*Ethics* (written during the early years of the war;
E, ¹1949) and the amazing visions of his last letters on the
"world come of age."

This is how Bonhoeffer himself describes the shift: "I thought
I could acquire faith by trying to live a holy life or something like
it. It was in this phase that I wrote *The Cost of Discipleship.*
To-day I can see the dangers of this book, though I am prepared
to stand by what I wrote" (*LPP,* p. 226).

In his earlier writings, Bonhoeffer was preoccupied with the
sociology of the church and with the consequences of faith in the
presence of Christ in his church, with "Christ existing as Christian
community," and with the distinctive nature of the community
in discipleship. In *Ethics,* however, his horizons are broadened
to include the Lordship of Christ not only in the church, but also
in the world. His concern now, obviously, is with the presence of
Christ in the center and in the fullness of life. He seeks to view
every sphere of life as part of the world reconciled in Christ with
God. In noting this change we do not mean to imply a breach
in Bonhoeffer's work as a whole. Nor will it be possible to quote
his latest thinking against his earlier theological essays. Rather,
we should draw the conclusion that it was the theology of the
earlier writings, the "ethical-social transcendence of God," the
"entering of God into reality" and the "vicarious action of
Christ," which now prove their worth when applied to other
themes. That is what causes the shift of which we spoke. The key
to the unity of Bonhoeffer's thought which underlies the various
themes in his writings may be found in this statement: "The more
exclusively we acknowledge and confess Christ as Lord, the more
freely the wide range of His dominion will be disclosed to us"
(*E,* p. 180).

The same christological concentration which characterizes the
earlier writings is found in the later writings, in *Ethics* and in
the *Letters.* But in these it takes the form of theocratic breadth,
as the Lordship of Christ extending into the midst of the world
in its secularity. Both belong together, like center and circum-
ference, proximity and horizon, concentration and expanse. As
we read in *Ethics:* "God's creation and God's kingdom are present

with us solely in God's self-revelation in Jesus Christ" (*E*, p. 60).

This christological affirmation, for all its exclusiveness, claims that in Christ the whole world as we know it is revealed *a posteriori* as God's creation, and, in the manner of prophecy and promise, as the kingdom of God. This dialectical relationship and dialogical tension between incarnation and creation, between cross and cosmic Lordship, must now be examined, at least in a preliminary way.

H. C. von Hase has drawn attention to the shift in Bonhoeffer's doctrine of the ministry or office (*Amt*).[1] Earlier Bonhoeffer had said that the communion of saints founded the "office." Now in *Ethics* he claims that the word of God establishes a clearly differentiated relation of superiority and inferiority. The preacher is not the spokesman of the congregation but, rather, the spokesman of God before the congregation. "This office is instituted directly by Jesus Christ Himself; it does not derive its legitimation from the will of the congregation but from the will of Jesus Christ. . . . at the same time it is *with* the congregation" (*E*, p. 259). The reason for this new conception of office is that the office of preaching, as distinct from the Christian life of the congregation, exists to serve Christ's total claim over the world in all spheres of life and not in the church alone. The word exercises its liberating and justifying service upon life in all its mandates —in marriage, labor, state, and church. For the office of preaching is not concerned with the word of the church or its dominion, nor with the sovereignty of God in the sanctuary, but rather with the cosmic dominion of the Reconciler of the world, which differs from it in its universality and totality. By serving this dominion of her master, the church takes her place in history in the time before the End, i.e., in the realm of the "penultimate." And she does so in the spirit of brotherhood, not of lordship, in the spirit of prophecy, not of clericalism, in partnership with the other mandates of God in the world of his creation. With this concept of office the church moves from the eschatological perfection into which it seemed to have fallen in Bonhoeffer's early writings into the realm of the "penultimate" and of the eschatologically provisional. Its commission is shaped by the dominion of Christ

[1] *EvTh* (1955), pp. 164 ff.

which transcends its own being and is limited by the mandates of Christ in the world, in which the whole world already stands, completely under the Lordship Christ claims, whether it knows it or not. From a methodological point of view the new shift in Bonhoeffer's thought might be described as a shift from his earlier, emphatically "church dogmatics" to a "theocratic theology." Theology thus becomes not only a "function of the church," but the function of the dominion of God as it was made manifest in Christ and is destined for the world.

Starting from Bonhoeffer's question about a "non-religious, secular interpretation of theological concepts," Gerhard Ebeling in "The Non-religious Interpretation of Theological Concepts" [2] is critical of the key words, "theology is a function of the church." Bonhoeffer's quest for a secular interpretation and for a secular expression of the Christian life begins at the very place of the Christian religion: "How can Christ become the Lord even of those without religion? If religion is no more than the garment of Christianity—and even that garment has had very different aspects at different periods—then what is a religionless Christianity? . . . How can we speak of God without religion, i.e., without the temporarily influenced presuppositions of metaphysics, inwardness, and so on? . . . In what sense are we in a religionless and secular sense Christians . . . not conceiving of ourselves religiously as specially favoured but as wholly belonging to the world? Then Christ is no longer an object of religion, but something quite different, indeed and in truth the Lord of the world" (*LPP*, pp. 163 f.).

1. THEOCRACY AND INCARNATION

This secular orientation of the doctrine of office in Bonhoeffer's *Ethics*, which we have just noted, suggests that his social ethics might be designated theocratic or, rather, christocratic. It is from his exegesis of Colossians 1, Ephesians 1, and Philippians 2 that he shapes his own peculiar view of the universal and ontological

[2] *Word and Faith*, trans. James W. Leitch (Philadelphia: Fortress Press, 1963), pp. 98–161.

aspects of theocracy in Christ. "In Jesus Christ the reality of God entered into the reality of this world" (*E*, p. 6). All conceptions of reality which do not take account of this entering of God into the world are abstractions, substitutions of a part of the truth for the whole. "Reality is first and last not lifeless; but it is the real man, the incarnate God" (*E*, p. 198). "To attempt to understand reality without the real man is to live in an abstraction to which the responsible man must never fall victim; it is to fail to make contact with reality in life" (*E*, p. 198). Henceforward one can speak neither of God nor of the world without speaking of Jesus Christ. "The reality of God discloses itself only by setting me entirely in the reality of the world and when I encounter the reality of the world it is always already sustained, accepted and reconciled in the reality of God" (*E*, p. 61). This language can, if you like, be understood in a realistic way. The language which Bonhoeffer uses to express this is, if you like, realistic and ontological, like the physical doctrine of the atonement in the early church. The incarnation is the statement about "objective" reality in the sense that there is a connection between God in Christ and all human life which is all-embracing and ontological, and prior to all human thinking, willing, and believing.[3]

In the cross this world is reconciled with God in its secularity. Faith can see the world and its secularity in every conceivable area of life, never in any other way, but always under this sign. "The reality of the world has been marked once and for all by the Cross of Christ, but the Cross of Christ is the cross of reconciliation of the world with God, and for this reason the godless world bears at the same time the mark of reconciliation as the free ordinance of God. The cross of atonement is the setting free for life before God in the midst of the godless world; it is the setting free for life in genuine worldliness" (*E*, pp. 26 f.). The reality which surrounds man, which makes demands on him and blesses him, is, as we have seen, not neutral, indifferent, or alien to faith. Far from it. In the light of the incarnation and the cross, understood at their deepest level, it is, in all its this-sidedness, God's reality. The difficult problems of act and being which had

[3] The same point is made by Karl Barth, *Church Dogmatics* III/4 (1961), pp. 39 f.; IV/2 (1958), pp. 275 ff.

engaged Bonhoeffer in his earlier writings are dropped. In their place we now have the exciting new concept of "reality" as the focal point. This can be understood only if its development from the personalistic thought of the early Bonhoeffer is taken into consideration. What he then termed "the reality form of the Thou" or the "social transcendence of God in the experience of the Thou" is further developed here to the point where the personal character of all of faith's experiences of reality is established: "Reality consists ultimately in the personal," Bonhoeffer says. He has just spoken of Holbein and how he personifies the sun, the moon, and the wind in his "Dances of Death." And he speaks of God incarnate as the one from whom all reality received its justification and its limits, origins, nature, and destiny (E, p. 195).

Bonhoeffer's magnificent thesis that God meets man, not when man is at the end of his tether but in the center of life (LPP, p. 191), is to be found as early as 1933 in his exposition of the tree of knowledge situated in the midst of paradise: *"Man's limit is in the middle of his existence, not on the edge.* The limit which we look for on the edge is the limit . . . of his possibilities. The limit in the middle is the limit of his reality, of his true existence. By the limit—the tree of knowledge—there is also the tree of life, that is, the life-giving Lord himself" (CF, p. 51). "Whoever professes to believe in the reality of Jesus Christ as the revelation of God, must in the same breath profess his faith in both the reality of God and the reality of the world; for in Christ he finds God and the world reconciled. And for just this reason the Christian is no longer the man of eternal conflict, but, just as the reality in Christ is one, so he, too, since he shares in this reality in Christ, is himself an undivided whole. His worldliness does not divide him from the world. Belonging wholly to Christ, he stands at the same time wholly in the world" (E, p. 67). This reconciliation unites the world and man. Here is freedom from the fear which is caused by differentiating between God's presence and the world's, a fear which drives man to flee from the claims of the world and to take refuge in the sacramental sphere of the church, or to flee from the claim of the divine command into conformity with the ways of the world or the forces of history. The reality in which believing man finds himself is—quite apart from his own belief or unbelief, consciousness or unconsciousness—the reality borne and accepted by God. This "entering of God into the world" is a real thing, a prior datum. And Bonhoeffer can emphasize it even to the point of saying: "in the events themselves is God" (*LPP,* p. 122). And we might continue, "Reality has a messianic character" (van Ruler). "Life knows now that it is held in tension between the two poles of eternity, that it extends from the choice made before the time of the world to the everlasting salvation. It knows itself to be a member of a Church and a creation which sings the praise of the triune God" (*E,* pp. 79 ff.). Thus each new life, as it is taken into and accepts the messianic reality, participates in the suffering of God in the world and joins in the joyful chorus of praise to God. Glentøj was right when he spoke of Bonhoeffer's "Faith in Incarnation and *anakephalaiosis*" (*MW* II, p. 199). With this we may compare *Letters and Papers from Prison* (p. 125): "The doctrine of the restoration of all things—ἀνακεφαλαίωσις—which is derived from Ephesians 1:10 *recapitulatio* (Irenaeus) is a magnificent conception and full of comfort." All this is not unlike the "Faustian character" of reality of which the early idealists spoke: "If it is God himself, who out of yearning for reality changes himself into nature, then the whole tumultuous plenitude of his destiny is in ferment beneath each current form of reality, and accounts for the Faustian character of life, which restlessly presses on from one reality to the next." [4] Bonhoeffer is really convinced that the incarnation has restored the whole of reality under one Head and that in Christ faith has a vision of the whole creation as it existed before God in the beginning and as it will be at the end.

All dualistic systems in terms of "realms" and "spheres" inevitably flounder upon this christological vision of the reconciliation of God and the world. So, too, does the scholastic differentiation between the natural and supernatural and the pseudo-Lutheran divorce of the two realms, and finally the separation of the enthusiasts from the world and, equally, the activism of the enthusiasts which opposes the world. This is how Bonhoeffer puts it: "The origin of action which accords with reality is not the pseudo-Lutheran Christ who exists solely for the purpose of sanc-

[4] H. A. Korff, *Geist der Goethezeit* II ('1957), p. 21.

tioning the facts as they are, not the Christ of radical enthusiasm whose function is to bless every revolution, but it is the incarnate God Jesus who has accepted man and who has loved, condemned and reconciled man and with him the world" (*E*, p. 199). And again: "Reality as a whole now falls into two parts, and the concern of ethics is with the proper relation of these two parts to each other. In the scholastic scheme of things the realm of the natural is made subordinate to the realm of grace; in the pseudo-Lutheran scheme the autonomy of the orders of this world is proclaimed in opposition to the law of Christ, and in the scheme of the enthusiasts the congregation of the Elect takes up the struggle with the hostile world for the establishment of God's kingdom on earth. In all these schemes the cause of Christ becomes a partial and provincial matter within the limits of reality" (*E*, pp. 62 f.).

In all these instances realities are dealt with without reference to the reconciliation of God and the world in Christ. In every case the unity and wholeness of reality thus restored are neglected and not achieved. Christ without the world, or the world without Christ, or man caught up in the eternal conflict between God and the world becomes the starting point for ethics. Human initiative can then no longer produce a synthesis or reconciliation. For the one synthesis of God and the world in the reconciliation wrought by Christ has not been accepted and can no longer be achieved. Bonhoeffer defies all tradition and boldly starts from "the one reality" and from "the whole reality" as it is given in the revelation of Christ, from which the miracle of cosmic reconciliation opens up. Of course, an apparently monistic conception like this is bound to raise suspicions. But we must remember that Bonhoeffer is certainly not thinking of a "unity as a matter of principle" as in the idealistic systems, but of the reconciliation of God and the world in the "person" of Christ. "It consists in Him as the one who acts in the responsibility of deputyship, as the God who for love of man has become man" (*E*, pp. 201 f.). Only when seen as coming from him and not from the world itself does the one and only reality become apparent, into which the believer sees himself translated. Such language cannot be derived from abstract theory or from everyday experience, but only by grasping the miracle of the incarnation. "Jesus Christ does not confront reality as one who is alien to it, but it is He alone who has borne, and experienced the essence of the real in His own body, who has spoken from the standpoint of reality as no man on earth can do, who alone has fallen victim to no ideology, but who is the truly real one, who has borne within himself and fulfilled the essence of history, and in whom the law of the life of history is embodied. He is the real one, the origin, essence and goal of all that is real, and for that reason He is himself the Lord and the Law of the real. Consequently the word of Jesus Christ is the interpretation of His existence and it is therefore the interpretation of the reality in which history attains its fulfillment. The words of Jesus are the divine commandment for responsible action in history in so far as this history is the reality of history as it is fulfilled in Christ, the responsibility for man as it is fulfilled in Christ alone" (*E*, pp. 199 f.). For this reason faith enters with him into the world of rediscovered unity and asks about "the way in which the reality in Christ, which for a long time already has comprised us and our world within itself, is taking effect as something now present, and towards the way in which life may be conducted in this reality. Its purpose is therefore participation in the reality of God and of the world in Jesus Christ to-day" (*E*, p. 62).

This is why Bonhoeffer will have no truck with the "battle cry" so beloved of contemporary Lutheranism: *regnum dei* and *regnum Christi* versus *regnum Satanae*. For it is just this same "wicked" world which is reconciled by God and for that very reason it is not the devil but Christ who is the ultimate reality (*E*, p. 70). For, as Bonhoeffer suggests, the clue to Luther is to be found not in the "tragic conflict between the two spheres" but, rather, in "the simplicity of the life which follows from reconciliation" (*E*, p. 301). Nor can there be any separation between the church and the world—an inference we might be tempted to draw from *The Cost of Discipleship*. For the church occupies a place in the world, not in order to deny the world a slice of its territory but as a witness to the world, telling it to remain the world—the world God has reconciled. This is to understand the world in its secularity and immanence better and more profoundly than it

understands itself according to its own lights. It explains why
Bonhoeffer can speak of the church of Christ as "the Church
of God and of the world."

2. THEOCRACY AND THE CROSS

This all-embracing Christocracy, unlike Byzantine theocracy,
does not find its image in the Holy Emperor. It is the dominion of
God in the person of the Crucified, i.e., dominion, authority, and
power in deputyship. "Christ helps us . . . by his weakness"
(LPP, p. 237). It is the act of vicarious representation which
lends color to the dominion of Christ, a dominion which is in-
comparable to all human life, and yet at the same time the likeness in which human life is destined to be molded. Bonhoeffer
takes up the Christology and ecclesiology of vicarious representation which he had worked out in Communion of Saints and develops it further in Ethics, applying it to all life created and redeemed by Christ for human fellowship under the mandates of
the world: "All His living, His action and His dying was deputyship. . . . Because He is life all life is determined by Him to be
deputyship" (E, p. 195). God's vicarious action in that unique
christological event "once and for all" is the ground and support
of life. Vicarious action of men for one another is the resultant
foundation of sociality in the mandates of marriage, labor, state,
and church, of their personal relationships as well as their relation
to things. The dominion of Christ manifested in deputyship—
because it is not an alien rule, but the dominion of the Creator,
Reconciler, and Redeemer—means liberation of human relations
in the family, labor, culture, and politics to become what they
were meant to be. The secular institutions become subject to
their own innate law for which they were created. This does not
mean that they are given an autonomy of their own. For that
would spell anarchy. Rather, they take their proper place in the
world in which God in Christ created, loved, and reconciled.
"Thus, under the dominion of Christ they receive their own law
and their own liberty" (E, p. 293).

Such are the implications of the Lordship of Christ for sin and its consequences, viewed in the light of his vicarious action on the cross. It does not mean that the secular orders are now made subservient to some human or religious ideal, to natural law or to the moral authority of the church. No, but "emancipated for true worldliness." Man can become man, the world can become the world, the state a state, etc. (*E*, p. 293). "The purpose and aim of the dominion of Christ is not to make the worldly order godly or to subordinate it to the Church but to set it free for true worldliness" (*E*, p. 294). Neither the separation of Christ and the world as in enthusiasm, nor the synthesis of Christ and the world as in Roman Catholicism, but the biblical doctrine of the dominion of Christ in vicarious action is the answer of the Reformation.[5] "The emancipation of the worldly order under the dominion of Christ takes concrete form not through the conversion of Christian statesmen, etc., but through the concrete encounter of the secular institutions with the Church of Jesus Christ, her proclamation and her life. By allowing this Church of Jesus Christ to continue, by making room for her and by enabling her proclamation of the dominion of Christ to take effect, the secular institutions attain to their true worldliness and law which has its foundation in Christ. Their attitude to the Church of Jesus Christ will always be a measure of the true worldliness which is not impeded by any ideological and alien law or by any arbitrary autonomy. A false attitude to the Church will always have as its consequence a failure to achieve genuine worldliness on the part of the secular institutions, the state, etc. and *vice versa*" (*E*, p. 294). The church's service to the world is, as it were, indirect. The church serves the dominion of Christ through its proclamation of justification and reconciliation. Life in the worldly mandates is emancipated from the terror of ideological self-justification to devote itself to genuine actions in the world, to fulfill its own particular destiny appointed for it by God.

For Bonhoeffer the dominion of Christ and "authentic worldliness" become interchangeable terms, once they are seen in the light of deputyship. Take also his positive understanding of the "world coming of age" and the "completely worldly life" in the

[5] So, too, from quite a different starting point, A. A. van Ruler, *Gestaltwerdung Christi in der Welt* (1956), pp. 35 ff.

last letters. This means in the final analysis only that the world has become world and man human as a result of their christocratic liberation from heteronomy and autonomy. Only the concentration of theocracy in the deputyship of Christ on the cross, in sin and reconciliation, opens up the horizons of a world come of age, restored before God to its primordial state and attaining its ultimate destiny. G. Ebeling [6] tries to develop Bonhoeffer's program for a nonreligious interpretation of biblical concepts in terms of the "theological category" of law and gospel: "Non-religious interpretation means interpretation that distinguishes law and gospel" (p. 141). But this attempt to bring some theological order into the question does not, in my opinion, get at the root of the problem as Bonhoeffer saw it. The problem of "religion" is whether the transcendence of God is epistemological or ethical. As for the interpretation of Western secularism, it is not really a matter of distinguishing between "hopeless" and "promising" types of godlessness. Nor is the basic structure of faith merely a matter of "enduring reality before God." [7] For Bonhoeffer the history of the growth of secularism in the West is a help to the true knowledge of Christ. It clears the decks of a false concept of God, and opens our eyes to the God of the Bible, who conquers power and space in the world by his weakness (LPP, p. 220). In this way it helps us to know "the dominion of Christ in cross and passion," in which emancipation for authentic worldliness is experienced. That—and not the application of the dogma of law and gospel —is the starting point for his vision of a "worldly interpretation" (LPP, p. 220). Bonhoeffer seeks to brink the worldly life of the Christian under the "total reality" of the dominion of Christ. That is why the biblical concepts can no longer be applied merely to the sphere of religion. This "worldly life" means not merely glossing over reality "with a veneer of religion," but a life of discipleship, following Christ and participating in the suffering of God in the world, "sharing in the life" of Christ (cf. LPP, pp. 222, 219).

The question naturally arises whether this "genuine" worldliness does not imply a new "Christian" worldliness. When the

[6] Op. cit., pp. 141 ff.
[7] Ebeling, op. cit., p. 160.

state becomes state, does this not imply, as Bonhoeffer sees it, a new kind of Christianizing of the state—so that in the last resort the world now come of age as a result of Western secularism, and emancipated from clerical or religious tutelage (cf. *LPP*, pp. 217 ff.), is after all, or perhaps for that very reason, understood by Bonhoeffer in terms of the Christian West. As a matter of fact, this is just what the chapter heading in *Ethics* (p. X) suggest (e.g., "The Foundations and Structure of a United West"). His ethical reflections have their own concrete place in history, which inevitably lies in the "Inheritance and Decay of the Christian West" (*E*, p. 25). Their task is to discover the shape Christ must take for our day to find in this the "Justification and Renewal of the Christian West." It is under these banners that the dominion of Christ takes shape in the history of the West today. This is where he marshals his thought, the complex of ideas associated with "genuine worldliness" as well as those connected with the "world come of age."

3. THE NEW CONCEPT OF REALITY

The real problem of ethics, and especially the problem of theology and jurisprudence, constantly flounders on the uncertain relationship between act and being, between the idealistic norms of natural law and the positivist apotheosis of reality. In the one case, the good is defined in terms of the ideal derived from an *a priori* "hierarchy of values" (N. Hartmann, H. Coing). In the other case, we are presented with a system of norms based on natural law and sanctioned by the church. In either case, the autonomy of the social process or the arbitrary development of human jurisprudence is itself the Good.[8] In his doctrine of reality, Bonhoeffer endeavors to find a breakthrough beyond what ought to be and what is, beyond idealism and positivism, beyond an ethic of norms and a social ethic, beyond natural law and positivist doctrine of law. To this overriding aim his *Ethics* is dedicated.[9] Basically, he

[8] Cf. K. Ritter's excellent exposition of this dilemma in philosophical jurisprudence, *Zwischen Naturrecht und Rechtspositivismus* (1956).
[9] Cf., e.g., *E*, pp. 107 ff., 292 ff., 326 ff.

seeks to grasp this peculiarly nebulous situation in christological terms: In Christ the reality of God has not become just an idea, value, or possibility for man, but has entered into his reality and into the reality of his world. In Christ the reality of the world is not just a *factum brutum* or in "naked facticity," but is accepted, reconciled, and so embraced by God. Thus Christian ethics does not deal only with the reality of the I or with the reality of the world over against the I. "But the problem of ethics at once assumes a new aspect if it becomes apparent that these realities, myself and the world, themselves lie embedded in a quite different ultimate reality, namely the reality of God the Creator, Reconciler and Redeemer" (*E*, p. 55). All things and relationships appear distorted when not seen and understood in God. "All so-called data, all laws and standards, are mere abstractions so long as there is no belief in God as the ultimate reality" (*E*, p. 56). "The problem of Christian ethics is the realization among God's creatures of the revelational reality of God in Christ just as the problem of dogmatics is the truth of the revelational reality of God in Christ. The place which in all other ethics is occupied by the antithesis of 'should be' and 'is,' idea and accomplishment, motive and performance, is occupied in Christian ethics by the relation of reality and realization, past and present, history and event (faith)" (*E*, p. 57). That is why Bonhoeffer can say: "Good is the real self. It is not the real in the abstract, the real which is detached from the reality of God, but the real which possesses reality only in God" (*E*, p. 57). So the tension is lifted between the norm and the *status quo* and there is no more need for the surrender of obligation to expediency. When reality is "materialized" as an idealism, it is as much an abstraction as is the so-called creative reality of positivism. Both notions are conceived in terms of the epistemological scheme of subject and object, not in the "sociological category" of Bonhoeffer's earlier writings. Thus both are limited by the "non-objectifiability" of human personality and the "non-subjectifiability" of man's sociality in his relationship with God and with his neighbor.[10] When reality is regarded in this light and made the object of faith, it becomes highly relevant for ethics: "Action which is in accordance with Christ is in ac-

---

[10] K. Ritter, *op. cit.*, pp. 58 ff.

cordance with reality because it allows the world to be the world; it reckons with the world as the world; and yet it never forgets that in Jesus Christ the world is loved, condemned and reconciled by God" (*E*, p. 200). This is the direction in which "the Christian is led . . . between the rigid bonds imposed by a system of standards authorized by the Church and the indifference *vis à vis* a self-evolving human jurisprudence which is autonomous, arbitrary and positivistic." [11]

4. THE COMMANDMENT

It should be clear that Bonhoeffer never sought the "ethical event" in direct encounters with reality or situations. Nor did he deduce it from a static system of ideal ordinances. Rather, it occurs for him at the point where the Lordship of Christ encounters man in the reality of the world. It is the encounter between God's dominion in his commandment and man's response. This means for Bonhoeffer: "The commandment of God is the total and concrete law to man by the merciful and holy God in Jesus Christ. . . . It is not the universally valid and timeless in contrast to the historical. It is not principle, as distinct from the application of principle. . . . God's commandment is the speech of God to men" (*E*, pp. 244 f.). God's commandment, in other words, comes in the unique, unpredictable, concrete situation, in the ethical event of encounter with God, in terms of reality as Bonhoeffer conceived it and as we have outlined it above. God's commandment is always concrete, seeking fulfillment in the real world of man.

As early as 1932 (see *No Rusty Swords*, pp. 163 ff.), Bonhoeffer makes everything depend on the concrete, prophetic character of the commandment and on its correspondence with reality. He warns against the church's habit of retreating in the crises of history from the concrete commandment, and contenting itself with issuing general guidelines and with proclaiming principles, pleading the lack of technical information: "The church cannot command without itself standing in faith in the forgiveness of

[11] E. Wolf, *Libertas Christiana* (Munich: C. Kaiser, 1959), p. 32.

sins. . . . What the sacrament is for the preaching of the Gospel, the knowledge of firm reality is for the preaching of the command. Reality is the sacrament of command" (NRS, p. 164, corrected). He never took up the point again. Yet it is important to notice the reason on which it is based: "The 'ethical sacrament' of reality is to be described as a sacrament only insofar as this reality is itself wholly grounded in its relationship of the reality of creation" (NRS, p. 164). In *Ethics* this sacramental language is dropped. Instead, Bonhoeffer writes: "The Decalogue is the law of living, revealed by God, for all life which is subject to the dominion of Christ" (E, p. 293). This is to hold firmly to the theology of the word and of faith against an easily misunderstood theory of the orders of creation. The commandment does not spring to light out of reality but it shines into created reality from above, from God's ordinance and appointment, as it was revealed in Christ. This means that God's commandment does not come to man when he is at his wits' end, where everything he had taken for granted becomes uncertain and unstable. Rather, it comes to him in the middle of life, embodied and set forth in the mandates he encounters here. And in the ethical event of the encounter with God, the mandates are revealed as divine institutions. God's commandment does not destroy created reality. It gives man the privilege and duty of living before God in the real, secular world. In such obedience, life before God becomes what it was really meant to be. Thus the commandment of God helps to emancipate created life in its various spheres from alien domination (heteronomy) and autonomy so that it can achieve that "genuine worldliness" which Bonhoeffer proposes to call "Christonomy." [12] What the commandment of God aims at producing in the train of the redemptive dominion of Christ is the cooperation of man, "participation in life and suffering" with God in the fullness of life in this world, giving and receiving the divine reality in the reality of the world, the "discipleship" of Christ in the obedience of faith. In sum, it means the integration of man into God's dominion over the world.

[12] E, p. 264, n. 1. For a similar view cf. P. Tillich, who sees in "theonomy" a way out of the autonomy between the clerical heteronomy of the Middle Ages and the secular autonomy of modern times.

This raises another question. Where is this divinely willed mandate encountered concretely and what authorities enforce it? Bonhoeffer finds the answer in his doctrine of the divine mandates. It is in them that he gives shape to the prophetic concretion of the one commandment of God for which he was searching in 1932 when he compared the commandment with the sacrament, in the manifold relationships of earthly life.

III.

The Mandates

1. THE TERM ITSELF

It is common knowledge that Bonhoeffer sets out twice in *Ethics* to discuss the idea of the mandates. On the first occasion he begins with the christological unity of reality (*E*, pp. 73 ff.). On the second occasion he starts with an inquiry into the factors that make ethical language possible and the translation of the law into concrete action (*E*, pp. 254 ff.).

1. The whole world is created through Christ and unto Christ whether it knows it or not. The world's relation to Christ takes concrete form in a number of divine mandates in which certain basic relationships and spheres of life are shaped and defined. "We speak of divine mandates rather than of divine orders because the word mandate refers more clearly to a divinely imposed task rather than to a determination of being."

With this we may compare *Ethics* (pp. 252 ff.). Here Bonhoeffer considers using the hitherto traditional concepts such as "institution," "estate," and "office." But he decides to drop them because of the historical misconceptions associated with them. "For lack of a better word, therefore, we will for the time being retain the term 'mandate,' but it is still our purpose, by dint of clarifying the concept itself, to help to renew and restore the old notion of the institution, the estate and the office" (*E*, p. 254). W. Künneth [1] finds here no more than a vindication of the use of the institutions. He fails to note the implications of Bonhoeffer's mandates for the rehabilitation of the whole concept of the institutions. Whether it was he rather than Bonhoeffer who introduced the "order of preservation" into the theological discussion in 1933 is another question which at least deserves notice. What was in Bonhoeffer's mind when he spoke of "order of preservation" (which is markedly different from that of Künneth in *Nation vor Gott* [1933])? This is a matter we will discuss a little later.

"It is God's will that there shall be labour, marriage, government and church in the world, each in its own way" (*E*, p. 73). The background of these statements is the controversy that was going on in the church and theology at the time of the Third Reich over the ideological glorification of race and nationality. In that controversy the principle of "national law" was invoked to justify and support the claims of the "German Christians." National law was the most important of all the institutions of creation. For Bonhoeffer this was a perversion of the doctrine of the institutions. Biology was being prostituted in the service of a political ideology. So he introduces the concept of the mandates and presses toward the God who lives and commands and who is revealed solely in the dominion of Christ. These orders are not demonic or divine forces in history, but definite demands and promises of God which demand obedient execution. "All the possible assertions with regard to secular institutions are founded upon Jesus Christ and must, therefore, be brought into relation with Him as the origin, essence, and goal of all created things. It is the dominion of Christ which renders all these assertions possible and significant" (*E*, pp. 292 ff.). "These institutions are, therefore, not a second divine authority, side by side with the God of Jesus Christ; but they are the place at which the God of Jesus Christ secured obedience to Himself. The word of God is

[1] *Politik zwischen Dämon und Gott* (Berlin: Evangelisches Verlagshaus, 1954), p. 136, n. 23.

not concerned with the institutions themselves, but with obedience in faith within these institutions" (*E*, pp. 322).

In this idea of the mandates as "the place where God secures obedience to himself" Bonhoeffer comes very close to the special ethics of Karl Barth.[2] The divine mandate, being the concrete place of faith and obedience, where a particular sphere on earth is claimed, taken possession of, and molded by the divine command, is removed from the dialectic of law and gospel. Much earlier, when speaking of the "call to discipleship," Bonhoeffer writes: "It is a gracious call, a gracious commandment. It transcends the difference between the law and the gospel" (*CD*, p. 49). The mandate is the place where the Christian works out the obedience of faith in the world. It has a directly evangelical content.[3] It shows the obedience of faith where it must exercise its responsibility. It shows a man where to love his neighbor. That is why the practice of the Christian life within the mandate means concrete obedience, as opposed to legalism.

There can be no doubt that the intention of Bonhoeffer's doctrine of mandates is to reformulate the original teaching of Luther about the "three primary powers" in which Christian sanctification is achieved, in cooperation with God in the world of suffering through "self-mortification." As Luther puts it in his sermon on "The Sacrament of Baptism": "Therefore God has instituted many estates in life in which men are to learn to exercise themselves and to suffer. To some has been commanded the estate of matrimony, to others the estate of clergy, to others the estate of temporal rule, and to all he has commanded that they shall toil and labour to kill the flesh and accustom it to death." "The three 'primary institutions' of social life in Christendom, viz., marriage, the state and the church, or alternatively family and economics, state and church, are founded by God. Even man can see how God has so ordered them that they correspond to nature.

[2] Cf. *Church Dogmatics* III/4 (1961), pp. 21 f.
[3] Cf. the teaching of Luther on the subject of the mandates: G. Wingren, *Luther on Vocation*, trans. Carl C. Rasmussen (Philadelphia: Muhlenberg Press, 1957), pp. 199 ff. "Man is free from the law, that he may heed the command. 'God's command' is of course in the service of the creatively new. It is a command given 'now' " (p. 231).

For they were created together with man. . . . they provide the
sphere where man may serve God in the world. They are what
Luther called 'the three primary powers to help us in resisting the
devil.' ("On the Councils and Churches," *Works of Martin
Luther* [Philadelphia: A. J. Holman & Company, 1931], p. 299.)
They are the 'natural law,' functions which have been established
in preparation for the coming of the kingdom of God and inseparably intertwined with one another. To that extent 'primary
power' is a better term than 'hierarchy' or 'estate.' The three
institutions to which we have reference are the church, the state,
and the economy. Two of them, it will be noted, are secular
powers, viz., the state and the economy. The 'secular state' in the
hierarchical structure of the *corpus christianum* (in Catholic
doctrine) is not left to itself on principle or made subject to the
'clerical estate' as a mere object of education. On the contrary,
their whole life is directly subject to the word of God." [4] This is
precisely the teaching which Bonhoeffer endeavors to refurbish.
And it is so much better expressed in his doctrine of the mandates
than in any theology of the orders.

This parallel is brought out well in J. Heckel's study of Luther.[5]
Life in the *ecclesia spiritualis* embraces all the activities and efforts
of the Christian, in whatever estate he may exercise his calling.
. . . In all three estates, in the three duties of the fifth commandment, in the three hierarchies the *officium omnis vitae* of the
Christian is performed.[6] "The hallmark of secular man is that
he is a Christian living in the world a life rooted in God, i.e.
the life which God himself lives in creation, in the estates and
offices of the created order. . . . Thus the Christian is a secular
man. He is not the co-creator but rather the co-operator in the life
of God, privileged to serve as the instrument of its realization."
This, then, is what the doctrine of the mandates involves: (*a*)
They are divine institutions, and because they are divine institutions they are discernible to faith, illuminated by revelation, and
point it to the place of obedience. (*b*) They were created together

---

[4] E. Wolf, *Peregrinatio* (1954), pp. 232 ff.
[5] "Im Irrgarten der Zwei-Reiche-Lehre," *ThEx*, N.F. 55 (1957), p. 53.
[6] Similarly G Törnvall, *Geistliches und weltliches Regiment bei Luther*
(1947), p. 171.

with man and so belong to the social structure of human existence in the world. (c) All of the mandates are embodiments of the one command and are therefore equal and inseparable from one another. They never lose their identity. They are *"larvae"* (Luther), means to an end and copies of divine realities. In them the life of the Christian here on earth is grounded in the life of God, in the life and dominion which God himself exercises and lives out in his creation. In them it is made plain to faith that "This is not a world we can rely upon but a world in which we may live a life of service" (Wingren, *op. cit.*, p. 44). "Perhaps we may speak here of a primordial or 'redeemed worldliness' as contrasted with the fallen world. This kind of worldliness has a representative and normative character." [7]

Wherever God's command confronts man in the moment of ethical decision the most important thing is to fulfill these mandates, using them as spheres for the practice of obedience. "This means that there can be no retreating from a 'secular' into a 'spiritual' sphere. There can be only the practice, the learning, of the Christian life under these four mandates of God. And it will not do to regard the first three mandates as 'secular,' in contradistinction to the fourth. For even in the midst of the world these are divine mandates, no matter whether their topic is labour, marriage, government or the Church" (*E*, p. 73). Thus the mandates serve—not on their own but in cooperation with and for each other, as God has coordinated them—to place man before the one and entire reality, the reality of the "body of Christ" (*E*, p. 77), in which God and the world are reconciled. Thus, finally, they help to set man free for "genuine worldliness" in the world and free to combat the fallen world. "The commandment of Jesus Christ does indeed rule our Church, family, culture and government, but it does so while at the same time setting each of these mandates free for the fulfilment of its own allotted function" (*E*, p. 264).

The mandates established in creation through Christ and attested in the biblical record of divine revelation are commissioned to carry out the commandment in all the departments of life. They are introduced into the world from above as articulations

[7] E. Wolf, *Peregrinatio*, p. 198.

of the dominion of Christ. They fan out as various expressions of
the sovereignty of God, and of the christological unity and wholeness of reality (E, p. 255). It is all centered on the person of
Christ. But the goal is a worldly life in obedience, suffering, and
the glorifying of God. That is how life in the world is restored
to its original and proper shape.

2. God's law presents itself concretely in the four mandates of
church, marriage and family, culture, and government. "The
commandment of God is not to be found anywhere and everywhere. It is not to be found in theoretical speculation or in
private inspiration, nor yet in historical forces or sublime ideals.
It is to be found only where it presents itself. The commandment
of God can be spoken only where God himself gives the warrant
for it, and only in so far as God gives the warrant for it can the
commandment of God legitimately be performed" (E, pp. 252 f.).
This is the second aspect under which Bonhoeffer views the mandates. It is not merely the intrinsically neutral "place of the obedience of faith." It is also the place, the office, the agency authorized
to proclaim, expound, and apply the commandment of God. It
challenges to obedience in specific cases. "By the term 'mandate'
we understand the concrete, divine commission which has its
foundation in the revelation of Christ and which is evidenced by
Scripture; it is the legitimation and warrant for the execution of
a divine commandment, the conferment of divine authority on
an earthly agent. The term 'mandate' must also be taken to imply
the claiming, the seizure and the formation of a definite earthly
domain by the divine commandment. The bearer of the mandate
acts as deputy in the place of Him who assigns him his commission" (E, p. 254)—the father toward his child, the teacher toward
the student, government toward the people, etc. Thus, the doctrine of the mandates does not imply unqualified sanctioning of
earthly rule. The mandates confer a commission to work out
what obedience requires in a particular earthly sphere. Equally
they confer a commission to carry out the commandment at a
particular time and place. In this second instance, the mandates
authorize and commission men to bear responsibility in certain
elemental situations in life. The mandates confer an authority

which is exercised in vicarious action for others. In the first instance the mandates are closer to the concrete "calling" than to the notion of a fixed profession or estate. Its aim is to produce the obedience of faith in various worldly spheres. In the second instance the emphasis is on the divine authorization to fulfill the commandment and with it to use the language of ethics in addressing other men.

This again fits in with Luther's doctrine of the *larva dei*: "Oportet enim Ecclesiam in mundo apparere. Sed apparere non potest nisi in larva, persona, testa, putamine et vestituto aliquo. . . . At tales larvae sunt Maritus, politicus, domesticus, Johannes, Petrus, Lutherus, Amsdorffius, etc." (WA Br. 9, 610.47).

As G. Wingren has commented: "If a statesman exercises his office in cooperation with God, he makes demands upon his subjects. Each *larva* for God is like this, an embodiment of the law: parents, neighbors, etc." [8]

2. THE ONTIC PRIORITY OF THE MANDATES

Bonhoeffer carefully chooses the term "mandate" in order to avoid a static institutional and spatial way of thinking. It would seem as though he brought forward only the imperative side, the act-character in human obedience, and therefore the historical aspect of the matter in question. In fact, he often comes pretty close to the English idea of "government" and to the doctrine of the call which R. Smend advocated during the earlier conferences of jurists and theologians. But when we remember Bonhoeffer's philosophy of reality and his earlier arguments in *Act and Being*, this initial impression proves to be misleading. True, the doctrine of the mandate emphasizes the element of God's kingly rule and "helps us to think of institutions as tasks to be molded by concrete decisions." [9] But it is clear that the mandates belong to the transcendent order of reality in the reign of God. They are prior to any human decision or choice and belong to the eschatological

[8] *Op. cit.*, p. 95; cf. E. Wolf, *Peregrinatio*, p. 233.
[9] E. Wolf, in *Recht und Institution*, p. 27.

sphere. "Amid the changes of all historical institutions these divine mandates continue until the end of the world" (*E*, p. 295). They are divine ordinances dependent on God's faithfulness to his covenant. They provide the pattern for the most elementary human relationships, regardless of their empirical origins. Although it is true that "if a concrete form of labour, marriage, government or church persistently and arbitrarily violates the assigned task, then the divine mandate lapses in this particular, concrete instance. And yet, through the divine mandate, what has concrete being acquires a relative justification" (*E*, p. 74). Empirical reality—i.e., the concrete forms of labor, marriage, government, and church—is so intimately bound up with the divine commission, that obedience to the mandate fulfills its original purpose while disobedience frustrates it.

At the same time the mandate-character of these elementary human relationships does not depend on their actual realization in history. It is, rather, a reality which consistently seeks fresh embodiment in empirical existence and even in opposition to it. Hence "mandate" is a flexible concept. It prevents any identification of the divine order with the *status quo*, expressing rather the living Lordship of God in commandment and obedience. Again, it is the direct antithesis to anarchy or *laissez-faire*, standing instead for the true and permanent character of the elementary human relationships, a character sanctioned by divine appointment. And all this regardless of whether or not they are realized in history. Thus the divine mandate confers a "relative justification" not only upon each successive act of obedience, but also upon the existing form of human relationships, which are sanctioned and appointed by the mandates. Thus neither tyranny nor insubordination can isolate a man ethically from the mandates. The son cannot be separated from the father, the husband from the wife, or the citizen from the state. The mandate imposes the necessity of sharing the burden and that "acceptance of guilt" (*E*, pp. 209 ff.), which Bonhoeffer emphasizes so passionately in the desperate situation of his time, and which he lived out existentially. Nor, on the other hand, can there be any question of moralizing the institutions. This has a particular bearing on the problem of a man's entry into or withdrawal from the institutions or mandates, e.g., by divorce or emigration or the like.

3. THE MANDATE AND THE PENULTIMATE: PREPARING THE WAY

Bonhoeffer coined the term "order of preservation" (*Erhaltungsordnung*) back in 1932 in contrast to the "order of creation" (*Schöpfungsordnung*), which was independent of the revelation of Christ. By this term he means the whole world order of fallen creation, "as directed solely towards Christ, towards the new creation" (*NRS*, p. 166). "The difference is this: With orders of creation empirical institutions are regarded as having an intrinsic worth, deriving from their primordial creation. They are 'very good.' 'Order of preservation' implies that each empirical institution is only preserved by God under his grace or wrath, awaiting the revelation in Christ. Every institution exists under the divine preservation, directed towards Christ and preserved for his sake alone. An institution is only to be considered part of the order of preservation so long as it is receptive for the proclamation of the gospel. Where an institution, even of the most elementary kind, like marriage, nation, etc., is fundamentally closed to this proclamation it must be abandoned. We must drop the idea of the order of creation, and look for the solution to ethical problems in general and to the ecumenical problem in particular in the divine revelation given in Christ." So Bonhoeffer once wrote in a memorandum (quoted in *MW* II, p. 133; cf. also J. Glentøj's controversy with W. Künneth, *ibid.*). In this same memorandum, which Bonhoeffer presented to Dr. W. A. Visser 't Hooft in Geneva in 1941, this new theory of the orders is developed further with the aid of the Decalogue: "A secular institution which abides by the decalogue will be receptive for Christ, i.e. for the church's preaching and for life according to his word. Such an institution may not be 'Christian' but it is a proper earthly institution according to God's will. . . . In the decalogue God revealed the limits which may not be transgressed if Christ is to be Lord of the world. The decalogue is framed in negative terms. The positive forms are brought out by living history, while the decalogue lays down the limits and provides a standard of judgment" (quoted in *MW* II, p. 190).

It is striking that in *Ethics* Bonhoeffer completely drops the term "order of preservation." Even the element of divine preservation of the world and through the orders is used only to a limited degree. In differentiation of "the last things and the things before last" (*E*, p. 79), he seeks a fresh approach to the subject by using terms unburdened with any previous associations. The justifying word is the final word of God in the qualitative sense of the *non plus ultra:* "There is nothing that goes beyond a life which is justified before God" (*E*, p. 81). But it also is the final word of God in a quantitative temporal sense: "It is always preceded by something penultimate, some action, suffering, movement, volition, defeat, uprising, entreaty or hope, that is to say in a quite genuine sense a span of time, at the end of which it stands" (*E*, p. 83). The penultimate must not be dispensed with for the sake of the ultimate, for it ensures the eschatological character of the eschatological. The dimension of the penultimate, of history, of exterior life is permeated, ordered, and arranged by the divine mandates. In these mandates God's final word receives concrete form and embodiment, life on earth its preparatory orientation for the revelation in Christ, and faith in the cooperation with God who is made flesh through love and good works. This period of the penultimate has its place in salvation history. It is extra time granted to prepare the way for the coming of Christ. Not that it is the condition of it. It simply shapes the present in the light of what is to come, and sanctifies existence in the world in justifying faith. Thus the penultimate becomes the "outer covering of the ultimate" (*E*, p. 90), the outer rim which surrounds the justifying Lordship of Christ and which is concerned with humanity and goodness, with "natural life" in expectation of the coming Lord and the coming kingdom. With this we may compare another statement in *Ethics:* "Only the triumphal entry of the Lord will bring with it the fulfillment of manhood and goodness. But a light is already shed by the coming Lord upon what is meant by being man and by being good in the way which is required for true preparation and expectation" (*E*, p. 96).

Standing in this time and in this space are the mandates—including the church—provisional in an eschatological sense. Under this earthly, physical covering of the ultimate, a world is to arise which is waiting for Christ, receptive to him and so serving him and glorifying him. Upon this sphere the light both of Christ and of his coming is shed, and also the shadow of the generation of Cain. Here is given a time and place for the mandates which "serve for the practice of Christian life." Within these limits the mandates are positive, godly institutions, bulwarks against chaos, but at the same time processes of integration, open to the coming of Christ.

Bonhoeffer refused to speak of "order of creation" because he saw that each worldly institution is founded by God. And because it is so founded, it can be recognized and appreciated only in the light of God's revelation in Christ and, in certain circumstances, is open to revision. He dropped the term "order of preservation," which at that time was equally open to misuse, because the preservation of the world is a rational notion, not identical with "relative justification" which experiences the penultimate and its institutions in the incarnation of Christ—the "entering of God" into the reality of the world. Moreover, natural life in the penultimate abhors any idea of ultimate purposes, even theological ones. The "natural" is not only the means to an end but an end in itself. In other words, it not only exists for Christ but Christ actually exists for natural life on this earth. To quote again: "In relation to Jesus the status of life as an end in itself is understood as creaturehood, and its status as a means to an end is understood as participation in the kingdom of God; while, within the framework of the natural life, the fact that life is an end in itself finds expression in the rights with which life is endowed and the fact that life as a means to an end finds expression in the duties which are imposed on it" (*E*, p. 107).

The "natural" is for Bonhoeffer "the form of life preserved by God after the fall" (*E*, p. 106). "It is already established and decided in advance, in the sense that the individual, the community and the institution all receive their allotted share in it" (*E*, p. 104). Therefore it cannot be justified in terms of the history of salvation as the "preservation" of the world and as a means to an end. It must not be understood as a preliminary stage for the life with Christ, for it receives its validation only from Christ himself. "Christ Himself entered into the natural life, and it is only through the incarnation of Christ that the natural life becomes the penultimate which is directed towards the ultimate. Only through the incarnation of Christ do we have the right to call others to the natural life and to live the natural life ourselves" (*E*, p. 102).

More recently E. Schlink has offered a new explanation for the secular institutions. When Bonhoeffer speaks of the "order of preservation" he is thinking of Luther's startling identification of Christ as the agent of creation with Christ as the agent of salvation: "He whom the world could never contain, lies in Mary's lap; he, who unaided sustains all things, has become a little child." [10]

So Bonhoeffer reinterprets Luther's concept of the *ordinationes* as *larvae dei*. He had already suggested as much when he claimed that the penultimate was the "outer covering of the ultimate" and that it was the destiny and sphere of the penultimate with the help of the mandates to promote the "practice of the Christian life." What Bonhoeffer is getting at comes out clearly when we compare it with the results of some of the modern studies of Luther. "It (sc. *iustitia civilis*) is neither preliminary of *iustitia christiana* nor its consequence. It is the place where the righteousness of God is realized by those whom he has justified within the 'estates,' as it is in the place where those 'good works' occur in which the *regnum Christi* prevails over the power of the devil '*in nostra imbecillitate*.' This is the life of 'discipleship' to Christ, and where it is achieved the Christian man recognizes 'the justification and therefore the righteousness of creaturely being' (Barth *Church Dogmatics*, III/1, p. 386)." [11] "The element of righteousness in *iustitia civilis* is none other than the righteousness of Christ, applied to the government of the world. Seen thus, *iustitia civilis* is not something alongside of *iustitia christiana* or alien to it, but on the contrary there is an organic connection between them. Therefore all the duties of Christians, such as loving one's wife,

[10] "Das Gebot Gottes, des Erhalters," *KuD* II (1956), pp. 256 ff.
[11] E. Wolf, *Peregrinatio*, p. 239.

rearing one's children, governing one's family, obeying the magistrate, etc., which they (sc. the Papists) regard as secular and fleshly—are fruits of the spirit. These blind men do not distinguish between vices and the things that are good creatures of God." [12] Again, as G. Törnvall puts it: "The righteousness of Christ is not concerned merely with the justification of the individual soul. . . . God sees the whole world cleansed by Christ. It is the constant mistake of scholasticism to make Christ into a private person. His work is meant for mankind as a whole. . . . Luther lays great emphasis on this point. . . . Scholasticism has been guilty of psychologizing the righteousness of Christ and of making it a human quality. The root of the trouble is that it ignored the christological perspective for which Christ is in the fullest sense God. The upshot of the christological approach is that Christ embraces the whole created world. Instead of which scholasticism has divided the divine and the human into an interior quality in the heart and preparatory natural righteousness respectively. We can see from this how Luther's criticism applies just as much to Protestant Orthodoxy. On the other hand civil righteousness must not be divorced from the created world, for it is the very thing that sanctifies creation. And conversely, the created world belongs to Christ. It is, if we may put it so, the robe which Christ wears." [13] Wingren says: "Associated with the idea of cooperation is that of the *larva Dei*. . . . Cooperation in his appointed calling makes man a *larva* for God at the point on earth where he stands." [14]

The best clue to help us understand why Bonhoeffer included the mandates in the realm of penultimate, in the "outer covering" of the ultimate, is to take his suggestion as an independent interpretation of Luther's statement—and, as the authorities on Luther quoted above would seem to show, the most fitting one: "Omnes ordinationes creatae sunt larvae Dei, allegoriae, quibus rhetorice pingit suam theologiam: sol alls Christum in sich fassen: ('should contain the whole Christ within itself.')" [15] It is against

---

[12] Luther, *Lectures on Galatians*, 1–4, trans. in *Luther's Works*, 26 (St. Louis: Concordia Publishing House, 1963).
[13] G. Törnvall, *op. cit.*, pp. 149, 150 f.
[14] G. Wingren, *Luthers Lehre vom Beruf*, p. 92.
[15] WA 40, I, p. 463; Comm. on Gal. 3:16.

this background that the christological foundation of commandment and mandate in Bonhoeffers' *Ethics* and his polemic against
the doctrine of the orders, which was so liable to be misconstrued,
must be viewed.

4. ANALOGOUS STRUCTURES

The doctrine of the mandates points to the positive intention of
the will of God toward the cooperation of man with God in the
service of the neighbor. At the same time it prevents us from
speculating about an immanent law of nature, of creation and of
preservation, whether self-authenticating or fixed by fate or
arbitrary appointment. But then we are bound to ask, Why are
these institutions divine mandates and not others? Bonhoeffer
speaks of four, sometimes five, mandates: labor, (culture), marriage, government, and church. How did he arrive at this selection?

1. These mandates serve a particular purpose which is grounded
in revelation and in the Bible, and they are under a divine
promise.

2. They are the place where the God of Jesus Christ produces
obedience for himself. They are institutions of God, ordained in
a manner corresponding to the reality of man, because they were
created together with him.

3. "It is perhaps not by chance that precisely these mandates
seem to have their type in the celestial world. Marriage corresponds with Christ and the congregation; the family with God
the Father and the Son, and with the brotherhood of men in
Christ; labour corresponds with the creative service of God and
Christ to the world, and of men to God; government corresponds
with the dominion of Christ in eternity; the state corresponds
with the πόλις of God" (*E*, p. 295).

It is noticeable that in this list of analogies the church is left
out, although Bonhoeffer includes it in the mandates.[16] Further-

---

[16] In Luther's doctrine of the three primary powers (*drey Ertzgewalten*), the
historical church of the cultus similarly finds its model and inner ground
in the *ecclesia spiritualis*. Cf. J. Heckel, "The Two Churches," *op. cit.*,
pp. 40 ff.

more it is typical that this list of analogies is not forced upon the reader but suggested as a vague reminder. It rests not upon analogy of being but upon analogy of relation between God's action and human action, between God's relations and human relations. This is how the principle of analogy must always be applied. It can never have the force of a category, whether it concerns thought, being, or action. The analogy of relation is concerned with the integration of human personality and sociality into the relationships of the trinitarian dominion of God. We need seek no objective proof for it. Rather, we must seek to enter into it and to appropriate it for ourselves. As we have seen, Bonhoeffer tried earlier in *Communion of Saints* to derive human personality from the I-Thou relationship and from the likeness to God there manifested. That led him to follow Tönnies in differentiating between "community" and "society." Community is eschatological and indissoluble. It stands in a genetic relationship to man's very being as a person. Society, on the other hand, is utilitarian, a temporal phenomenon which only partially affects the human person. Social life cannot be credited with the ability to mold human personality. Although this distinction is somewhat questionable, it does lend color to Dombois's attempt to divide and categorize the institutions as typical forms of relationships according to whether they are *a priori* or existential.[17]

5. DEPUTYSHIP OR VICARIOUS ACTION

The law of God endows the mandates with irreversible relationships of superiority and inferiority above and below, which are independent of empirical relationships of power. In establishing this hierarchical arrangement, it confers the warrant for ethical discourse, of which we have spoken, and for the execution of the divine commandment (*E*, p. 246). "In Bonhoeffer's doctrine of the mandates, is there not just a suggestion of North German patriarchalism?" asks Karl Barth on this point.[18] This impression may not be accidental, and both Bonhoeffer and Barth may be at

[17] Cf. H. Dombois, "Das Problem der Institutionen und die Ehe," in *Recht und Institution*, pp. 55 ff.
[18] *Church Dogmatics* III/4 (1961), p. 22.

fault. All the same it should be noted that Bonhoeffer is not talking of a purely external authority derived from an official position, but an authority which is existential and personal, resting upon self-sacrifice and vicarious action for others. Just as through Christ every human life is destined for deputyship and responsibility, so, too, are the human relationships in the mandates by the very action of accepting them in deputyship, in being-for-others on an empirical level. The concrete acceptance of deputyship and responsibility for the neighbor is obedience under the divine mandates. That, and that alone, creates those irreversible interhuman relationships within the mandates: Christ and humanity, church and world, father and child, government and citizen, man and things. In substance the mandates are not derived from the Platonic ideas. Rather, the life of obedience within them means "being-for-others" in discipleship to Christ. It is in the living out of this kind of deputyship as a disciple that there are within the mandates cooperative tendencies between complementary though dissimilar entities, functions, and offices, as is obvious from the example of the family, or the state, or in labor relations. The imperative structure of the mandates thus rests upon the indicative structure of deputyship, whether the latter is already present or still to be achieved.

6. THE COORDINATION OF THE MANDATES

It is the will of God to use the mandates to establish the sovereignty of his commandment over the whole world and over all of human life, yet concretely, in the appropriate way for each mandate. Each mandate is subordinate only to the christocratic unity of reality and derives from thence its own dignity and authority. The mandates are not in competition with one another, nor can they be deduced from any one single mandate. Thus there cannot be any separation between church and secular mandates, but only a division of function, each limiting and complementing the other. Nor can the spiritual hierarchy be made superior to the natural or secular orders. For the church exists in the world as a divine mandate alongside the others. All men stand together under all of the mandates equally, and only in its totality does "humanity" stand before the whole earthly and eternal reality, the reality which God has prepared for it in Jesus Christ (*E*, pp. 67 f.). All of the mandates are expressions of the one commandment of God, despite their differences. Hence they are not self-sufficient, nor can one mandate establish a dictatorship over the others: "The authorization to speak is conferred from above on the Church, the family, labour and government, only so long as they do not encroach on each other's domains and only so long as they give effect to God's commandment in conjunction and collaboration with one another and each in its own way" (*E*, p. 246). The supremacy of the commandment of God is shown precisely by the fact that the relative authorities of the mandates are coordinated. They are complementary and parallel, existing side by side in association and opposition, and it is only in this multiplicity of concrete correlations that the one dominion and authority of God over the whole world can take effect. The secret of this multiplicity is the multiplicity of the dominion of God and of the whole of reality in Christ. This implies:

1. That the kingdom of Christ is not confined to the church. The church is its mandate, its *larva*, its herald in the sphere of the penultimate. The church's Lord is the Lord of all the world or else he is not Lord over his church.

2. That within the period of the penultimate each mandate is a mandate in subordination to and in partnership with the other mandates. Each mandate has its concrete historical limitations, being protected and encouraged to perform its own allotted task in the sight of God by the other mandates. Only in such reciprocal limitation and complementation can they express the sovereignty of Christ in its entirety. "The commandment of Jesus Christ, the living Lord, sets creation free for the fulfilment of the law which is its own, that is to say, the law which is inherent in it by virtue of its having its origin, its goal, its essence in Jesus Christ. The commandment of Jesus does not provide the basis for any kind of domination of the Church over the government, of the government over the family, or of culture over government or Church, or for any other relation of overlordship which may be thought of in this connection. The commandment of Jesus Christ does in-

deed rule over Church, family, culture and government; but it does so while at the same time setting each of these mandates free for the fulfilment of its own allotted functions" (E, p. 264).

This coordination of the mandates strikes me as a specially felicitous thought of Bonhoeffer's. Each mandate is bounded on two sides: by the eschatological reign of Christ, so far as its existence and function is concerned, and by the other mandates in regard to its limits. This applies especially to the church, with its temptation to clericalism (the hierarchical principle), and to the state, with its tendency to ideological totalitarianism (state-church, etc.). As to the precise functions the mandates are required to perform, that is something for history to decide. It is a matter for constant debate and determination over specific issues, such as family rights, education, etc. But their coordination, corresponding to the task they have to fulfill, will always remain. This is a line of thought which Bonhoeffer develops in connection with the Lutheran doctrine of the three estates, or rather the "three primary powers." Their essential feature and abiding significance, as he sees it, lie in their complementary character rather than in the domination of any one of them over the others. The secular order is protected from an alien ecclesiastical domination and *vice versa*. This is well brought out in a passage from *Ethics*: "With regard to the relationship of the secular institutions to one another and to the Church, the Lutheran doctrine of the three estates, *oeconomicus, politicus* and *hierarchicus*, has as its decisive characteristic and permanent significance that it is based on coordination rather than any kind of priority and subordination, so that the worldly order is safeguarded against alien rule of the Church, and *vice versa*. In my opinion this doctrine must be replaced by a doctrine which is drawn from the Bible, the doctrine of the four divine mandates, marriage and family, labour, government and Church. These institutions are divine in that they possess a concrete, divine commission and promise which has its foundation and evidence in the revelation" (E, pp. 294 f.). Luther writes: "Omnes status huc tendunt, ut aliis serviant. Mater custodit puerum; ipsa non indiget, sed puer. Vir cogitur surgere: posset domire, sed quia uxorem et pueros nutrire cogitur, idea surgendum.

Nos omnia invertimus." [19] Similarly Wingren: "Each estate exists to serve the others. . . . Thus the estates themselves are ethical subjects for the estate is God working through the law." [20] The doctrine of the three estates in Luther and in later Protestant Orthodoxy arose from the reshaping and declericalization of the medieval *corpus christianum*. That is why Protestant Orthodoxy has always been inclined to use the scholastic theory of natural law as a means of giving expression to the doctrine. Bonhoeffer, however, tries to develop a biblical doctrine of the four mandates. True, he is not uninfluenced by the empirical form Christ has taken in the West. But still, the primary question is what Scripture has to say about the function of these mandates, and about the promise for them.

If we are drawing up a "table of institutions," this scheme of Bonhoeffer's is a much better guide to begin with than a new edition of the traditional Lutheran doctrine of the three estates. And this, despite the fact that Bonhoeffer takes over Luther's original view of the "three primary powers" and subjects it to further development.

7. THE SPECIFIC FUNCTIONS OF THE MANDATES

a) For Bonhoeffer the mandate of labor includes property, culture, and society. It has a supra-lapsarian basis in the biblical command "to dress it and keep it" (Gen. 2:15). It deals with man's integration into the creative dominion of God, a creation of things, values, and relationships based on the world God has created: "By this means there is created a world of things and values which is designed for the glorification and service of Jesus Christ. This is not a creation out of nothing, like God's creation; it is a making of new things on the basis of the creation by God. No man can evade this mandate. From the labour which man performs here in fulfilment of the divinely imposed task there

[19] WA 15, p. 625, 7.
[20] *Op. cit.*, p. 18. On the coordination of the estates in Luther, see further E. Wolf, *Peregrinatio*, pp. 232 ff.

arises that likeness of the celestial world by which the man who recognizes Jesus Christ is reminded of the lost Paradise" (E, p. 75). "But it is the race of Cain that is to fulfil this mandate, and that is what casts the darkest shadow over all human labour" (E, p. 75). The world of the penultimate is permeated by this mandate. Although the shadow of Cain casts a gloom across fulfillment, yet for the believer there is even here an analogy, a reminder and foretaste of the original and eschatological final being in the world before God. All labor is also "responsibility for things" (E, p. 196), and thus bears the character of deputyship, quite apart from its social significance.

b) The mandate of marriage includes both marriage and family and has the same supra-lapsarian basis. Man is integrated into the creative dominion of God through the procreation and education of children. In this partnership in God's sovereign rule the believer discerns an analogy with the "marriage betwixt Christ and his church." Marriage and family life provide an eminent example of life in deputyship.

c) The mandate of government presupposes—and this is important—the mandates of labor and marriage. The state finds these mandates already in the world for whose order, protection, and rule it is responsible, and is itself dependent upon them. Government serves to protect the world of labor in society and culture and to protect marriage and family. It can never make itself the subject of the world of labor or of family life; otherwise it would destroy its own presupposition and in doing so destroy itself. Government is designed to watch over life and protect it, and is thus designed for deputyship (E, p. 297). By accepting deputyship it derives its authority from God in exercising its function and also—a relative measure—its historical shape. "Its own authority is only a form of the authority of Christ" (E, p. 311). "As a citizen a Christian does serve in a different way" (E, p. 311). To the extent that the dominion of the state is integrated into the dominion of Christ, the Christian believer perceives in it an analogy, a reminder and reflection of the dominion of Christ which is present, hidden and still to come in manifest form. Service to the state is a part of true human life in the sight of God. The art of statesmanship is an essential part of a life which "corresponds to reality" and is lived responsibly (*E,* p. 326).

d) The mandate of the church is to proclaim the revelation of God in Christ. Wherever Christ is proclaimed in accordance with the divine mandate, there is always a congregation. In its proclamation the church serves justification, and thereby the emancipation of all human life across the board through all mandates: "The cross of atonement is the setting free for life in genuine worldliness" (*E,* pp. 262 f.). The reign of Christ thus proclaimed by the church is in no case the domination of the church over the natural, worldly institutions. Because the church is one mandate among others, Bonhoeffer differentiates the church's universal proclamation of the gospel from the law of the church as a social community, and as a public body with a life of its own, distinct from secular institutions. "The word of God, proclaimed by virtue of the divine mandate, dominates and rules the entire world; the 'community' which comes into being around this world does not dominate the world, but it stands entirely in the service of the fulfilment of the divine mandate" (*E,* p. 265). The congregation serves the mandate laid upon it in a twofold manner, in the double relationship of deputyship. "The Christian congregation stands at the point at which the whole world ought to be standing; to this extent it serves as deputy for the world and exists for the sake of the world. On the other hand, the world achieves its own fulfilment at the point at which the congregation stands. The earth is the 'new creation,' the 'new creature,' the goal of the ways of God on earth. The congregation stands in this twofold relationship of deputyship entirely in the fellowship and disciplehood of its Lord, who was Christ precisely in this, that he existed not for his own sake but wholly for the sake of the world" (*E,* p. 266).

e) The last letter of Bonhoeffer from prison, dated January 23, 1944 (*E,* p. 253, n. 1), contains the following passage on friendship: "Friendship is not easy to classify in this scheme sociologically. Marriage, labour, the state and the church each have their concrete, divine mandate. Its place is not in the domain of obedience but in the free expanse of liberty which encompasses the three domains of the divine mandates. A man who has no knowledge of this free expanse of liberty may be a good father, a

good citizen and a good worker and no doubt he may also be a
good Christian; but I rather doubt whether he is a complete
human being; and to this extent I doubt also whether he can be
a Christian in the full meaning of the term. Our 'Protestant (not
Lutheran) Prussian world' is so completely governed by the four
mandates that these entirely overshadow the free expanse of
liberty." [21] This led Bonhoeffer to consider whether the church
is not the place for the rediscovery and revival of "aesthetic
existence." The Christian, like ethical man, recognizes the claim
of the law; but the Christian is further impelled by the spirit of
divine sonship. For that very reason, therefore, he should know
something of the free expanse of liberty, beyond the limits of
duty and purpose. Like a field full of cornflowers, obedience to
the four mandates should be surrounded and accompanied by the
sphere of freedom (*LPP*, p. 125).

It seems to me that this view of freedom is part and parcel of
the doctrine of obedience and the mandates. For what Bonhoeffer is aiming at in his idea of the mandates is a comprehensive
view of life as a whole. He wants to find out what life really
means to be. He is utterly opposed to any systematization or one-
sidedness. The citizen who keeps himself to himself—the manager,
the politically active man, the monk—is an impoverished being,
a caricature of humanity. He cannot live a full life, deeply involved in the world and yet constantly aware of death and resurrection. Only by a comprehensive embodiment of all these aspects, each complementing the others, is a sociology under the
sign of reconciliation in Christ meaningful or productive.

Finally, let us glance at the critical appreciation of Karl Barth
on Bonhoeffer's doctrine of the mandates.[22] Barth considers Bonhoeffer's essay a more helpful development than the thought of
Althaus and Brunner. For as he sees it, "What is involved in the
constancy of ethical events must also be learned only from the
Word of God if a formed reference to it is to the legitimate and
meaningful." [23] Yet, Barth claims, Bonhoeffer does entertain a few
arbitrary notions, among which he mentions:

---

[21] Cf. J. Huizinga's analysis of culture, *Homo ludens* (Boston: Beacon Press,
1955).
[22] *Church Dogmatics* III/4 (1961), pp. 21 ff.
[23] *Ibid.*, p. 22.

1. The arbitrary selection of the mandates. It is not always clear what the biblical justification for them is.

2. His onesided analysis of them as involving "the authority of some over others" in which any idea of the freedom of the inferior *vis à vis* superior personages is conspicuous by its absence.

3. The definition of constants in human relationships as "mandates" which are hardly distinguishable from "command": "Is it not the case that the reference to these relationships as such does not necessarily have the character of an imperative, and therefore in the strict sense of a mandate, but that it must become an imperative, a concrete command or mandate, in the power of the divine command itself, in the ethical event." [24] As Barth sees it, in *Ethics* Bonhoeffer has advanced beyond the theory of the order of creation but he is still somewhat confined within the thought forms of that doctrine. For Barth, on the other hand, the issue at stake is "that in which the Word of God tells us at this point we are merely referred to certain constant relationships as such," [25] which do not have the character of an imperative. They are in truth "spheres," though not "laws." [26] But, we might ask, are there not still on the periphery of ethical events such neutral spaces and areas, like the outlines of a stage, where ethical events are acted out? That is the question. Do not these neighborly relationships regain their original function in the light of the word and faith as "definite historical forms" (*E*, p. 245) of the domains of Christ in the commandment? Bonhoeffer is not concerned to demonstrate the relationship between the mandates for their own sake. He does want to demonstrate the structures of christological unity in reality. But it seems to me his real problem is the "warrant for ethical discourse" and the "execution" of the divine commandment in the world. The question is not what these relationships are in themselves, but what they have to say and what is to be said through them in connection with the ethical event of the word.

But are those "structures" in reality constructions which dam up the living stream of divine history into a reservoir? Bonhoeffer saw the limitations of the doctrine of the mandates. As early as

---

[24] *Ibid.*
[25] *Ibid.*
[26] *Ibid.*, pp. 30 f.

The Cost of Discipleship he wrote: "The limits . . . of the secular calling are fixed by our membership of the visible Church of Christ" (pp. 239 f.). His discussion in *Ethics* (pp. 222 ff.) of "vocation as the place of responsibility" ends in a dilemma. There is always the possibility of conflict between concrete historical vocation and the accompanying perception of responsibility, on the one hand, and the limits drawn, on the other, by the law of God as revealed in the Decalogue, and by the historical forms of the mandates of marriage, labor, government, and church. Bonhoeffer's answer to this conflict between one law and another is as follows: "It is precisely responsible action which will not separate this law from its Giver. It is only as the Redeemer in Jesus Christ that responsible action will be able to recognize the God who holds the world in order by his law; it will recognize Jesus Christ as the ultimate reality towards which it is responsible and it is precisely by him that it will be set free from the law for the responsible deed" (*E*, p. 229). Here we may be able to derive a final nuance from the mandates. The negative rigidity which has been the object of complaint might be removed by integrating them into the living history of God. And then, finally, we shall see the law in the hand of the Lawgiver and the mandate in the hand of the God who commissions men to his service.

Jürgen Weissbach

CHRISTOLOGY AND ETHICS

I.

Introduction: The Method of Approach

Throughout his life Dietrich Bonhoeffer was concerned with commandment and action, with right behavior and the Christian life. It would therefore be natural to follow the theme through his works in chronological order and to structure this essay accordingly. This is the method of procedure in most studies of Bonhoeffer.[1] Encouraged by Jürgen Moltmann's essay, "Die Wirklichkeit und Gottes konkretes Gebot, nach Dietrich Bonhoeffer" ("The Reality of the World and the Concrete Law of God according to Dietrich Bonhoeffer"[2]), I have decided upon two courses. First, I shall follow a systematic line, dealing with various themes which to me seem especially to illuminate Bonhoeffer's ethical principles. Then I shall hope to throw more light on Bonhoeffer's later thought, including his works on special ethics. Like Karl Barth, Bonhoeffer regards dogmatics and ethics as a unity, following the tradition of Reformation theology. Consequently, all his systematic works are slanted toward a concern for ethics.[3] In following this scheme I consider it imperative to

[1] On the method of Bonhoeffer interpretation, cf. Gisela Meuss, "Arkandisziplin und Weltlichkeit bei Dietrich Bonhoeffer," MW III, pp. 68–70, where the most important discussions on method are listed. Cf. also J. Moltmann, above, pp. 21 f.
[2] In MW III, pp. 42–67.
[3] Cf. on "Ethics and Dogmatics," Karl Barth, Church Dogmatics I/2 (1956), pp. 875 ff. and II/2 (1957), pp. 543 ff. I shall attempt, with the limitations indicated above, to take this into account as far as possible.

check back into the derivation of Bonhoeffer's thought in his earlier works, as well as to note the changes and developments it underwent in the later phases of his work. And I hope—despite this systematic treatment—to avoid reducing it all to a single level. Bonhoeffer's emphases vary at different periods of his life. There are even some contradictions in his thought; but I think they can be explained in part in the light of the various situations to which he speaks, and in part by the variety of subject matter.[4]

II.

Bonhoeffer's Theology and Ethics: The Starting Point

Bonhoeffer, following the Reformation tradition, takes as his starting point the revelation of God in Jesus Christ. He refuses to start with any man-made premises or questions, an attitude which permeates his whole theology even to the "nonreligious interpretation." In general terms he makes this point in *Act and Being*: "From God to reality, not from reality to God, goes the path of theology" (AB, p. 89). This statement already shows how seriously he takes the condescension of God in Christ, even though he does not say it in so many words. In his lectures on Christology he makes the point explicitly in christological terms.[1] "Nothing

---

[4] Cf. especially J. Moltmann, above, pp. 55–58; he rightly rejects the view that there was any breach in Bonhoeffer's thought.

[1] Despite a certain hesitation I consider it permissible to quote from *Christology*, which was put together posthumously from notes. Cf. C, pp. 17 f.

can be known of either God or man before God has become man in Jesus Christ" (*C*, p. 105).[2] During the period of his Tegel imprisonment[3] we find the same appeal, but with a stronger ethical orientation: "It is necessary to free oneself from the way of thinking which sets out from human problems and which asks for solutions on this basis. Such thinking is unbiblical. The way of Jesus Christ, and therefore the way of all Christian thinking, leads not from the world to God but from God to the world" (*E*, p. 320). Thus Bonhoeffer's thinking starts with the revelatory act of God in Christ, or, from the human point of view, with justification. This is especially true of his *Ethics*.[4]

Granted Bonhoeffer's theology starts with the event of revelation, this must on no account be taken to imply a "supra-naturalistic positivism of revelation,"[5] for, to use Karl Barth's phrase, he has the "horizontal"[6] in view. The same principle permeates all his works, beginning with his use of sociological categories in *Communion of Saints* to interpret and explain the church, and that despite the fact he understands its nature from the event of revelation.[7] It comes out a little later in his use of the Antaeus saga in the Barcelona lecture of 1929.[8] As Eberhard Bethge has observed, "Bonhoeffer could not let Nietzsche have a monopoly of loyalty to the earth" (*GS* III, p. 7). Finally it comes out in his key words, "the world comes of age" in the *Letters and Papers from Prison*. Thus Bonhoeffer is able to formulate a program for ethics in these terms: "the way in which Christ takes form among us *here and now*" (*E*, p. 23).[9] Bonhoeffer is concerned in his ethics to avoid both "relativizing revelation" and "relativizing the his-

[2] Cf. also the letter to Rüdiger Schleicher, dated April 8, 1936, GS III, pp. 26 f.

[3] On the possibility of the word of the church to the world, *see E*, pp. 318 ff. For the dating cf. Eberhard Bethge, *Ethik* (German ed. of 1963), p. 17.

[4] Cf. Karl Barth, *Church Dogmatics* II/2 (1957), p. 546.

[5] J. Moltmann, in MW III, p. 45.

[6] Cf. Karl Barth, *Church Dogmatics* III/4 (1961), p. 17.

[7] Cf. H. C. von Hase, "Begriff und Wirklichkeit der Kirche in der Theology Dietrich Bonhoeffers," MW I, pp. 26–45, especially p. 28.

"What Is a Christian Ethic?" Lecture in Barcelona, January 25, 1929, in (Tegel) NRS, pp. 39–48; cf. further GS III, p. 494.

[9] Italics mine–J.W.; in Bonhoeffer the whole quotation is printed in italics.

torical, the norms of creation" (GS III, p. 35).[10] In this connection he refers with approval to Karl Barth.[11] He "has actually
attempted, on the strict Reformation principles, to avoid relativizing the historical. It is very persuasive. In a thoroughly Biblical
way he relates all orders of the created world exclusively to Christ,
asserting that they can be understood only through him and must
inevitably find their fulfilment only in him" (GS III, p. 35). Here,
in outline, is Bonhoeffer's main concern, especially in regard to
ethics. It is my hope to fill in the picture in the following pages.

III.

Basic Social Concepts and the Principle of Deputyship

Bonhoeffer introduces the concepts which are so important to
his ethical writings quite early in his dissertation *Communion of
Saints*.[1] These are: the I-Thou relationship; individual and collective personality; and person and society. Here he does the all-
important spadework for his *Ethics*, as will be demonstrated again

[10] Letter to Gerhard and Sabine Leibholz, dated March 7, 1940, GS III,
pp. 33 ff.
[11] On the relationship between Bonhoeffer and Barth, cf. Moltmann, above,
and Regin Prenter, "Dietrich Bonhoeffer und Karl Barths Offenbarungs-
positivismus," MW III, pp. 11–41. [The English-speaking reader should
consult the index of NRS s.v. "Barth, Karl" (Trans.).]

[1] On Bonhoeffer's place in the history of theology, on the evolution of his
dissertation, and on the context of the concepts to be discussed here in the
history of theology and philosophy, cf. Gerhard Ebeling, "Nonreligious Interpretation of Biblical Concepts," *Word and Faith*, trans. James W. Leitch
(Philadelphia: Fortress Press, 1963), pp. 98–161; H. C. von Hase, MW I,
pp. 26 ff.; and especially Moltmann, above, pp. 21–55.

and again from many different angles. All the way through, the concept of deputyship is of central importance.

1. THE "PERSON" IN *COMMUNION OF SAINTS*

In *Communion of Saints* Bonhoeffer develops his distinctively Christian concept of the person. He does it in controversy with the philosophical concept of person, and specifically with the pattern of subject and object (*CS*, pp. 25 ff.) beloved of idealism, in connection with the "I-Thou relationship" and with the "basic social category" (*CS*, p. 37). "So the Thou form (the "alien subject" [*CS*, p. 28]) is to be defined as the other who places me before a moral decision" (*CS*, pp. 33 f.). "This is a purely moral (not an epistemological) transcendence, which is experienced only by the man who makes a decision" (*CS*, p. 33). "For it is only with the Thou that a person arises" (*CS*, p. 35). "The I arises only with the Thou; responsibility follows on the claim" (*CS*, p. 36). "But this seems to make a man the creator of the other's moral person" (*CS*, p. 36). That, however, is something which no man can do on his own. "God, or the Holy Spirit, comes to the concrete Thou; only by his action does the other become a Thou for me, from which my I arises. In other words, every human Thou is an image of the Divine Thou" (*CS*, p. 36).[2] "The other man is Thou only insofar as God makes him his" (*CS*, p. 36). The Christian person arises always anew: "The person is continually arising and passing in time" (*CS*, p. 30). With this should be compared another passage in the same work: "In the 'moment' the individual again and again becomes a person through the 'other.'" Bonhoeffer is inquiring into the person in sociological relationship (*CS*, p. 37).

Since, in the other Thou, I encounter the divine Thou, my way to him is like the way of faith to God, the way of recognition or rejection. "But since I first know God's I in the revelation of his love, so too, with the other man. . . . Then it will become clear that the Christian person achieves his true nature when

[2] This passage is italicized by Bonhoeffer.

God does not confront him as Thou, but 'enters into' him as I"
(CS, p. 37). Here we meet the christological concept of the entry
of God which is so crucial for Bonhoeffer, especially in *Ethics*.[3]

Thus, in the final analysis, Bonhoeffer's concept of the person
has a christological basis in the incarnation. This applies equally
to the principle of deputyship, a point which is brought out
clearly in this passage from *Act and Being*: "But through the
person of Christ the I's fellow-man is also rescued from the world
of things, to which he of course continues to belong *qua* entity,
and drawn into the social sphere of persons. Only through Christ
does my neighbour confront me as making some form of absolute
claim on me from a position outside my own existence. Only
here is reality sheer first-hand decision. Without Christ my very
neighbour is no more than my possibility to self-assertion through
'sustaining his claim' (Grisebach)." But this is not to be misunderstood in a psychological sense: "There is the limit for
psychology and epistemology, for the personal being of the other
is a moral reality which cannot be grasped by psychology as a fact
or by epistemology as a necessity" (CS, p. 35).[4] On pages 34 f.,
above, Moltmann draws a distinction between Bonhoeffer's personalism and that of Gogarten: "But Bonhoeffer parts company
with Gogarten at a crucial point." This is where "Bonhoeffer
starts thinking in christological and ecclesiological terms" (above,
p. 34). (The reader will find further bibliographical material on
the subject of personalism there as well as on p. 29 n. 10. See
W. Pannenberg, article on "Person" in RGG[3], vol. V, col. 230 ff.
and further bibliography there). In *Communion of Saints* Bonhoeffer restricts his application of insights to the doctrine of the
church: "The christological grounding of humanness and human
relations, which in Bonhoeffer's earlier writings is applied to the
community of Christ in the church. Later in *Ethics* it refers to
the 'larvae' of God that we meet in the world. It is obvious how
close Bonhoeffer is to Karl Barth's christological interpretation of

---

[3] Cf. J. Moltmann, above, p. 33.
[4] For a critique of Kierkegaard's individualistic concept of the person, cf.
Chapter II, n. 8, CS, p. 211, as well as J. Moltmann, above, pp. 33 f. And
for a critique of Karl Barth's *Epistle to the Romans* see notes on Chapter
V, n. 47, p. 226, CS, and J. Moltmann, above, p. 35.

man's relations to his fellow men" (Moltmann, above, p. 35). How close Bonhoeffer's understanding of the person comes to that of Luther is shown in Ernst Wolf's interpretation of Luther's *De libertate christiana:* "Luther ventures to suggest that the Christian is a 'Christian' only to the extent that he appears to others in Christ. Phil. 2:5 ff., which was used by the early church as the basis for its dogma of the two natures, in order to elucidate the problem of the divine-human person of Christ, is expounded by Luther directly to mean the Christian man in the world (26, 25 ff.). Truly Christian living is the voluntary imitation of Christ's self-humiliation." [5]

2. THE CONCEPTS OF COMMUNITY IN *COMMUNION OF SAINTS*

From the concept of the person Bonhoeffer arrives at the concept of community, the race and the collective person.[6] Bonhoeffer postulates an "equilibrium between personal and social being" (*CS,* p. 50). "We maintain that the community can be understood as a collective person, with the same structure as the individual person" (*CS,* p. 50). He seeks to forestall any false individualism: "God created man and woman, each dependent on the other. God does not desire a history of individual men, but the history of the community of men" (*CS,* p. 52).

The human race is pictured as made up of individual "self-conscious and self-acting" persons (*CS,* p. 78). For the doctrine of sin this means that "everything clearly depends upon finding [7] the general act in the individual's sinful act without making the one the basis for the other. An ethical category must be related to the individual as an individual person. Man is the race precisely in being the individual" (*CS,* p. 79).[8] In princi-

---

[5] Ernst Wolf, "Libertas christiana und Libertas ecclesiae," *EvTh* 9 (1949–1950), 1.139; the numbers in the quotation apply to the page and lines in *De libertate christiana* according to J. Svennung, *Kleine Texte für Vorlesungen und Übungen,* ed. H. Lietzmann, No. 164, 1932.

[6] On these concepts see Moltmann, above, p. 37.

[7] Printed in italics in the original.

[8] Cf. Moltmann, above, pp. 39 f.

ple none of us is distinct from Adam (*CS*, p. 79).[9] The nature of sinful man, however, is a duality: it is a collective person and "yet subject to endless fragmentation. This duality is its nature, annulled only by the unity of the new mankind in Christ" (*CS*, p. 85).[10] With this we may compare a passage from *Act and Being* (p. 165): "It is not in terms of historicalizing theories, psychologizing interpretations, that the structure of Adam's humanity should be conceived; rather should it be thus regarded: I myself am Adam, am I and humanity together; in me falls humanity; as I am Adam, so is every individual, but then in all individuals the one person of humanity, Adam, is active" (cf. also *CF*, p. 77). Here Bonhoeffer's personalism acquires its deepest foundation, viz., in the action of Christ. Whereas the old humanity is fragmented into many Adams, "which are conceived as a unified entity only through each individual, the new mankind is completely drawn together into the one single historical point, into Jesus Christ, and only in him is it comprehended as a whole" (*CS*, pp. 106 f.). Here we meet the important concept of deputyship, which permeates all the auxiliary concepts that Bonhoeffer borrows from social philosophy.[11] In Jesus Christ, God took humanity—not just a single man—upon him. "But because the whole of the new mankind is really established in Jesus Christ, he represents the whole history of mankind in his historical life" (*CS*, p. 107).[12]

This insight can be traced throughout Bonhoeffer's works. I quote from *Ethics*: "Whatever happens to Him, happens to man. It happens to all men, and therefore it happens also to us. The name Jesus contains within itself the whole of humanity and the whole of God" (*E*, pp. 10 f.). In Jesus who dies as a sinner, bearing the sin of the world, love triumphs in deputyship and thereby guilt is actually punished and overcome (*CS*, p. 112). In his vicarious action Adamite humanity is transformed into Christ-

---

[9] Cf. the use of the concept "monad" in the section of *CS* dealing with social philosophy (*CS*, pp. 15–21).
[10] Printed in italics in the original.
[11] Following Moltmann's translation, above, pp. 43 f. Cf. a further observation of Bonhoeffer himself: "It contains deep problems of social philosophy" (*CS*, pp. 113 f.).
[12] In the original, part of this quotation is in italics.

humanity once and for all. In this event of incarnation and justification lies the profoundest basis for Bonhoeffer's doctrine of
person and community, a basis which is strictly christological.

3. THE ROLE OF DEPUTYSHIP IN
BONHOEFFER'S ETHICS

This definition of person and community, which is derived in
the last analysis from the vicarious act of Christ, is of major importance for the whole of Bonhoeffer's theology. Here I would like
to concentrate mainly on the doctrine of deputyship in Bonhoeffer's ethical writings, and bring out its implication for the new
man, for ethical action, and for freedom and love.

In *Communion of Saints* the doctrine of deputyship has definite
implications for ethical acts within the congregation, the *Christus
praesens* who stands as deputy for all humanity. "My dealings
with him take place on the basis of the life-principle of vicarious
action" (*CS*, p. 107). This happens in three different ways: in
the support of the neighbor in active love, in intercession, and in
the forgiveness of sin. Of course, this is not something that anyone
or everyone can do. "The idea of vicarious atonement is possible
only so long as it rests upon an offer of God, that is, it is in force
only in Christ and in his church. It is not a moral possibility or
standard, but solely the reality of the divine love for the church;
it is not a *moral* but a *theological* concept" (*CS*, p. 114).[13]

In *Creation and Fall* this personalistic approach is applied to
the doctrine of the *imago dei* in connection with human freedom.[14] Bonhoeffer defines freedom in terms of relationship. "Being free means 'being free for the other,' because the other has
bound me to him" (*CF*, p. 35). Freedom is not a substantial,
individualistic concept, but is realized only in the event of my
being bound to the other.[15] Freedom is not derived from creation
but has a christological basis: "It is the message of the gospel that

[13] Italics mine–J.W.
[14] For Bonhoeffer's doctrine of the *imago dei* and in particular his use of the
analogy of relationships and the analogy of being, cf. Karl Barth, *Church
Dogmatics* III/1 (1958), pp. 185 ff. and J. Moltmann, above, pp. 53 f.
[15] This is the way Bonhoeffer almost invariably defines it; cf. *E*, p. 194.

God's freedom has bound us to itself, that his free grace only becomes real in this relation to us, and that God does not will to be free for himself but for man. God in Christ is free for man. Because man does not retain this freedom for himself the concept of freedom only exists for us as 'being free for' " (*CF*, p. 35). In speaking of God's being "bound," Bonhoeffer even at this early date indicates that freedom is not to be misunderstood in an activistic sense.

The idea of "being . . . for," which Bonhoeffer derived from Christology, colors the whole of his theology. Let me quote a few more passages to prove the point: "In revelation it is a question less of God's freedom on the far side from us, i.e. his eternal isolation and aseity, than of his forth-proceeding, his *given* word, his bond in which he has bound himself. . . . God is not free *of* man but *for* man. Christ is the Word of his freedom. . . . Here a substantial [understanding] comes to supplant the formal understanding of God's freedom. If it should prove itself it will suggest redirection of our attention from revelation seen in terms of the act towards ontological ideas" (*AB*, pp. 90 f.). On the question of freedom and the contingency of revelation, and on the unity of act and being which is given in Christ and present in the church in accordance with the idea of the *Christus praesens* there are further observations in *Christology*. Let me quote one section from it: "But the decisive element in the *pro me* structure is that the being and action of Christ are maintained within it. *Actio Dei* and *praesentia Dei*, the being *for you* and *being* for you, are combined when the unity of act and being in Jesus Christ is understood in this way, the question of his person, i.e. the question 'who?', can be rightly put. He is the one who has really bound himself to me in free existence. And he is the one who has freely preserved his contingency in his 'being there for you.' He does not *have* the power of this being *pro me*, he *is* this power" (*AB*, pp. 90 f.).

Bonhoeffer applies the same idea to the elements of the sacrament: "As elements of the restored creation they are of course nothing in themselves, but for men. This being-for-men is what makes them a new creation. The Christ present in the sacrament is the creator of this new creation, and is at the same time a creature" (*AB*, p. 59). Again, it is in connection with the theology of the cross in *The Cost of Discipleship* that we find the word "representative" (deputy).[16] As H. Müller has observed: "*The Cost of Discipleship* is a church-oriented ethics. It is neither an ethics dealing straightforwardly with the profane act of men in society and in nature in a way corresponding to earthly reality, nor with Christian Ethics, 'the realization among God's creatures of the revelational reality of God in Christ'" (*E*, p. 57). Church ethics is, rather, the question of the reality of the justification of the sinner in his obedience, of the reality of faith in grace and of works done through grace.[17]

Again, to quote Ernst Wolf, "Bonhoeffer's treatment of discipleship is hardly pietistical. But its main preoccupation is with the individual as a member of the congregation, and with the limits of the church's involvement with the world. He has not yet linked up discipleship with mission. Much more prominent, for the moment, is the picture of the church as a pilgrim people on its way through the world, suffering under the sign of the cross."[18] The church is the body of Christ, sharing his cross and passion. Like Christ, who took upon himself guilt and sin, so the church bears the suffering and sin of the world." As it follows him beneath the cross, the church stands before God as the representative of the world" (*CD*, p. 82). It cannot do this in its own strength, but only because it is supported by Christ. The individual is to be for his neighbor an *alter Christus*. The christological foundation of this and its proximity to the earlier writings is obvious.[19]

The theology of deputyship plays an all-important part in *Ethics* and in *Letters and Papers from Prison*. The lines are pro-

[16] On the origin of *The Cost of Discipleship*, cf. especially Karl Barth, *Church Dogmatics* IV/2 (1958), pp. 533 f.; G. Meuss, *MW* III, p. 74; and E. Bethge's review of Hanfried Müller, *Von der Kirche zur Welt*, *MW* IV, p. 171. G. Meuss, H. Müller, and Ernst Wolf substantially agree in their judgment of *The Cost of Discipleship*.

[17] Hanfried Müller, *Von der Kirche zur Welt* (Leipzig: Koehler und Amelang, 1961), p. 197.

[18] E. Wolf, "Was heisst Königsherrschaft heute?" *BevTh* 32 (Munich: C. Kaiser, 1961), p. 73; cf. also G. Meuss, *MW* III, p. 75.

[19] Bonhoeffer's affinity with Luther at this point is self-evident; cf. above, Chapter III, n. 6. For the christological basis see *CD*, p. 81.

longed, with a stronger relevance toward the world. Compare, e.g., the following passages: "In this real deputyship which constitutes His human existence, He is the responsible person *par excellence*, because He is life, all life is determined by Him to be deputyship" (*E*, p. 195). "But we are called into this same love to the whole world, a love which has been sealed by the cross of Jesus" (*GS* III, pp. 476 f.). As far back as 1932 Bonhoeffer had related these thoughts more closely to the world (even then deputyship had universalist implications). In the lecture delivered on November 19, 1932, "Dein Reich komme" ("Thy Kingdom Come") he insists on the church's continuing solidarity with the world (*GS* III, p. 276). In *Communion of Saints* he repudiates Scheler's version of solidarity, as we may see from the following quotation: "Not 'solidarity,' which is never possible between Christ and man, but vicarious action, is the life-principle of the new mankind. I know, certainly, that I am in a state of solidarity with the other man's guilt, but my dealings with him take place on the basis of the life-principle of vicarious action" (*CS*, p. 107).[20]

In the lecture of February 4, 1932, delivered at the School of Technology in Berlin and entitled "On the Right of Self-Assertion" he says of man "that he does not consider himself lord of his own life" but, rather, "considers himself responsible for his brother-man. Here he does not live alone but essentially through and for the other, in a relationship of responsibility for him" (*GS* III, p. 265). Here, again, the idea of deputyship is grounded in the event of justification; though, as I see it, it has here a wider human application. "He offers the sacrifice of mankind by which alone mankind can live, and since Golgotha the whole of mankind finds the source of life in what the Son of Man did when he offered up himself to the Father for his brethren" (*GS*, III, p. 269). He remarks at this point, too, that the church as the new humanity stands in deputyship before God. With this we may compare two passages from *Ethics*: "What takes place in her

[20] More recently Ernst Wolf has again taken up the idea of solidarity in his article on "The Meaning of the Lordship of Christ Today" (*BevTh* 32, pp. 67 ff., especially p. 72, the passage from which the foregoing quotation was taken, and p. 85).

takes place as an example and substitute for all men," and "The congregation of Jesus Christ is the place at which Christ is believed and obeyed as the salvation of the whole world" (*E*, pp. 21, 208). Like Christ, the church bears the guilt of the world, though not as an additional burden. This takes concrete shape in the confession of sin, which springs from justification, a confession unreserved and entire, calling men to join in it (cf. *E*, pp. 50 f.). Hence there is laid upon the church a twofold responsibility: "for Christ before men and for men before Christ" (*E*, p. 193).

It is in connection with the confession of guilt that Bonhoeffer's personalism proves extremely helpful. The church is "precisely that community of human beings which has been led by the grace of Christ to the recognition of guilt towards Christ" (*E*, pp. 46 f., 48). Within the church are "innumerable individuals, each of whom must in this way be conscious of being to blame for the whole. For indeed these innumerable individuals are united in the collective personality of the Church. It is in them and through them that the Church confesses and acknowledges her guilt" (*E*, pp. 46 f., 48). On the other hand, these suggestions lead to vicarious action. This vicarious action is Christlike action and therefore the only kind of behavior that is truly realistic.[21] It is "based on the reality of deputyship created by the fact God made man in Jesus Christ for mankind." So it is understandable that "Jesus is not concerned with proclamation and realization of new ethical ideals. . . . He is concerned solely with love for the real man" (*E*, p. 208). When he wrote *Communion of Saints* (pp. 118 ff.), Bonhoeffer already realized that love was not (primarily at any rate) just a humanitarian notion, a vague feeling of sympathy or eroticism (*CS*, p. 121), but human love completely absorbed into the will of God for man (*CS*, p. 124). It is an appointment and gift of God. The same view occurs again in *Ethics*: "Everything that we have so far seen to be true excludes all those definitions which endeavour to represent the essence of love as a human attitude, as conviction, devotion, sacrifice, the will to fellowship, feeling, brotherhood, service, action" (*E*, p. 172). Love is recognizable only in the light of the revelation of God in Christ. It is strictly christological and personal: "Only in Jesus Christ do

[21] Cf. especially "Ethics as Formation," *E*, pp. 3 ff.

we know what love is, namely in His deed for us" (*E*, p. 173). And again: "Love is not what it *does* and what he *suffers*, but it is what *he* does and what *he* suffers" (*E*, p. 174). This is an important clue for Bonhoeffer's thought: the work does not interpret the person, but the person interprets the work.[22] Thus love is not just an idea but a person. Like freedom, the love which is so important to ethics is a concept deduced from Christology. This is the reason why it is not "self-righteously high-principled action" (*E*, p. 213); nor does it imply immunity from bad behavior (*GS* III, p. 469). Although our behavior is poisoned by original sin, it is relatively sinless because it participates in the "action of Jesus Christ" (*E*, p. 213). Where the church refuses to bear the guilt of others and to live for them, it ceases to be the church. The same is true of the individual Christian: "If I refuse to bear guilt for charity's sake, then my action is in contradiction to my responsibility which has its foundation in reality" (*E*, p. 214). In Christ, who is life, there is only life in deputyship. That is the only kind of responsible existence.[23]

In *Letters and Papers from Prison* the key words "concern for others" (*LPP*, p. 237, etc.) and "the Church for the world" became more prominent.[24] Once again it is impossible to misunderstand these suggestions in a moralistic way. Like everything we have noted hitherto, they are grounded in Christology. The very use of the word "participation" (*LPP*, p. 237) shows that. Although Bonhoeffer does speak of Christ as an "example" (*Vorbild*, in quotation marks in the German original), we can be quite sure that he did not mean an imitation-piety, for he goes on to base it on the incarnation: "[it] has its origin in the humanity of Jesus" (*LPP*, p. 240). "This concern of Jesus for others [is] the experience of transcendence" (*LPP*, p. 237) he says in his tirade against the religious misunderstanding of Christian faith.[25] "Faith

---

[22] Cf. *C*, pp. 44 f.; *CF*, pp. 19 ff., 32 f.; *GS* III, p. 237; *CD*, pp. 54 ff.

[23] On the limits to which one can go in bearing the guilt of others, cf. Chapter V, below; on the significance of deputyship for the doctrine of the mandates see below, p. 143.

[24] At the time of his arrest a note was found in his desk with the words "to be for the world" (E. Bethge, *Ethik*, ⁶1963, p. 16). The quotations are all taken from "Outline for a Book" (*LPP*, pp. 256 ff.).

[25] Cf. Chapter III, section 1, above.

is participation in this Being of Jesus (incarnation, cross and resurrection)" (*LPP*, p. 237). This other is "the nearest Thou to hand" (*LPP*, p. 238, corrected). Jesus is "God in human form," not "autonomous man" but "existing for others, and hence the Crucified" (*LPP*, p. 238). Here once more are the characteristic key words, providing the clue to the christological sources of Bonhoeffer's thought: vicarious action, incarnation, and crucifixion. In carrying out her mission the church "must take her part in the social life of the world, not lording it over men, but helping and serving them" (*LPP*, p. 239). "She must tell men, whatever their calling, what it means to live in Christ, to exist for others" (*LPP*, p. 261). That ethical behavior is grounded in Christology from start to finish ought to be clear by now.[26]

IV.

Christ and the Reality of the World Where Christian Life Is Lived

In his Barcelona lecture Bonhoeffer says: "Ethics is a matter of history, it is not simply something which has descended from heaven to earth, but it is rather a child of earth" (*NRS*, p. 40). The importance of reality for Bonhoeffer's ethics can be demon-

---

[26] This is substantiated to my mind successfully by G. Ebeling in *Word and Faith*, *op. cit.*, pp. 98 ff., and even more by R. Prenter in his essay "Bonhoeffer und der junge Luther" ("Bonhoeffer and the Young Luther"), (*MW* IV, pp. 33 ff.). Both of these writers show that nonreligious interpretation has a christological basis in the theology of the cross.

strated all through his works. As he put it in his lecture, "A Theological Basis for the World Alliance?": "What the sacrament is for the preaching of the Gospel, the knowledge of firm reality is for the preaching of the command. Reality is the sacrament of command".[1] In Tegel, in a discussion of the concretion of the law, Bonhoeffer states: "If one speaks of God one must not simply disregard the actual given world in which one lives; if one does that one is not speaking of the God who entered into the world in Jesus Christ, but rather some metaphysical idol" (pp. 326 f.).[2]

How does Bonhoeffer regard those realities which are so essential for the Christian life, viz., nature, the world, institutions, etc., in relation to Christ? In other words, does he define the dominion of Christ? In dealing with this question I shall rely mainly upon *Ethics*. Bonhoeffer's Christology as it concerns our problem is based largely on texts like Philippians 2:6 ff.; Colossians 1:15 f.; Ephesians 1, but also on John 1; Hebrews 1; 1 Corinthians 8:6; 2 Corinthians 8:9; etc.[3] His Christology, as the lecture on Christology makes abundantly clear, is determined by the Lutheran doctrine of condescension (cf. especially C, pp. 110 f.). For him the decisive question is the person of Christ. He is the God-man. He is not concerned with how this should be so, but maintains it as a paradox all through. Christ is present in word, sacrament, and congregation.

These passages introduce the relevant concepts of mediation, creation, incarnation, crucifixion, reconciliation, resurrection, glorification, and the Lordship of Christ. The Christ event in its complex unity provides the basis for reality and hence for ethics as well.[4]

---

[1] NRS, pp. 157–173. Quotation from p. 164, corrected. For this period the lecture "Thy Kingdom Come" is also to be noted. Cf. the Antaeus passage (above, p. 91) and the discussion of the sacrament of the law and the problem of concretion (GS I, p. 34) in a letter to Erwin Sutz (1932).
[2] "What is meant by 'Telling the Truth'?" (E, pp. 326–334). On the dating, cf. E. Bethge's Foreword in Ethik (⁶1963).
[3] In CD there is an almost complete list of the relevant passages (CD, p. 212).
[4] Cf. Karl Barth, Church Dogmatics III/4 (1961): "We have reliable and legitimate information about this horizontal by God's Word or not at all."

1. JESUS CHRIST, THE MEDIATOR OF CREATION

"All created things are through and for Christ and exist only in Christ (Col. 1:16). This means that there is nothing, neither persons nor things, which stands outside the relation to Christ" (*E*, p. 288).[5] Christ is the mediator of creation and therefore its center.[6] "Because all created things exist for the sake and purpose of Christ they are all subject to Christ's commandment and claim" (*E*, p. 288). "It is in vain to seek, to know God's will for created things without reference to Christ" (*E*, p. 262). The Lordship of Christ embraces the whole universe.

2. CREATION AFFIRMED IN THE INCARNATION

God does not abandon his creation, despite its corruption by the fall, nor his claim upon it. On the contrary, Christ becomes "*the* new creature" (*C*, p. 66). The favorite expression for the incarnation all through *Ethics* is, "God enters into created reality" (*E*, p. 89), which embraces mankind, history, nature, in short, τὰ πάντα.

J. Moltmann points out[7] that the same idea occurs in the Protestant theology of German idealism, e.g., in Richard Rothe. It can be traced even to Bonhoeffer's earliest works. Later, in his elucidation of the *imago dei*, Bonhoeffer uses the phrase in *Creation and Fall*: "Here created freedom means—and it is this that goes beyond all previous deeds of God, the unique *par excellence*—that God himself enters into his creation" (*CF*, p. 36). Again in the same work he writes, "God glorifies himself in the body: in this specific form of the human body. For this reason God enters into the body again where the original in its created

---

[5] Cf. very similar sayings in *CD*, pp. 84, 212, and in *E*, pp. 73, 288, 252, 295, 301 f.

[6] For more on the idea of the center, see Chapter V, below.

[7] *MW* III, pp. 46 f.

being was destroyed. He enters it in Jesus Christ. He enters into it where it is broken, in the form of the sacrament of the body and of the blood".[8] Similarly, in "Thy Kingdom Come" he says: "We live in the accursed field, which bears thorns and briars, but— Christ has entered the accursed field; the flesh, which Christ bore, was taken from this field" (GS III, p. 273). It means for him that God has identified himself with the world. Any statement made about the world which disregards this event is an abstraction. God has himself accepted the created order. This leads Bonhoeffer to the exaggerated statement, ". . . In the events themselves is God" (LPP, pp. 122 f.).[9] Notice, however, the period when this was written (letter of January 23, 1944) and the "pastoral concern"; "Whatever weakness, self-reproach and guilt we contribute to these events, in the events themselves is God. If we survive the next few months, we shall be able to see quite clearly that all has turned out for the best" (LPP, pp. 122 f., corrected). But Bonhoeffer was no pantheist. That would be to misunderstand him, as I shall hope to show later on. God did not become simply identical with the created order. Bonhoeffer's "faithfulness to the earth" has a christological basis in the incarnation.

The upshot for Bonhoeffer is that any gnostic or idealistic spiritualization, any "detestation of the body" is out of the question. "The escape from the created work into bodiless spirit, into mind, is forbidden. God wills to look upon his work, to love it, to call it good and preserve it" (CF, p. 22). "It is from this point of view that the body is conceived as the prison from which the immortal soul is released for ever by death. According to Christian doctrine, the body possesses a higher dignity. Man is a bodily being, and remains so in eternity as well. Bodiliness and human life belong inseparably together. And thus the bodiliness which is willed by God to be the form of existence of man is entitled to be called an end in itself" (E, p. 112). Yet any distinction between personal and real ethos is equally impossible: "The will of God is directed not only to the new creating of men, but

---

[8] CF, p. 46; cf. also C, pp. 66 f.
[9] J. Moltmann, in MW III, 46.

also to the new creating of conditions." [10] "Nothing is in principle an adiaphoron" (*E*, p. 292). The person must not be isolated from the world of things; that was the sin of idealism: "Christ does not detach the person from the world of things but from the world of sin; there is a great difference. There are no things 'in themselves,' which are not related to the person" (*E*, p. 291). The dominion of Christ must not be abandoned over any sphere of life (*E*, p. 292). [11]

In addition to the passages on the incarnation and the mediatorial function of Christ, Bonhoeffer finds a further christological basis for this in the doctrine of the restoration of all things in Christ, which he derived from Ephesians 1:10. For the later Bonhoeffer this theology of recapitulation acquired considerable importance. It is the background of his statements in *Ethics*. The only explicit references to Ephesians 1:10 and the theology of recapitulation are in *Ethics* (p. 288) and in *Letters and Papers from Prison* (pp. 114 f.). I quote the passage from *Letters and Papers from Prison*: "What does 'bring again' mean? It means that nothing is lost, everything is taken up again in Christ, though of course it is transfigured in the process, becoming transparent, clear and free from all self-seeking desire. Christ brings it all again as God intended it to be, without the distortion which results from human sin. The doctrine of the restoration of all things— ἀνακεφαλαίωσις—which is derived from Eph. 1:10, *recapitulatio* (Irenaeus), is a magnificent conception, and full of comfort." [12]

3. JUDGMENT AND RECONCILIATION

Even the incarnation itself contains an element of judgment, for Jesus was Man without sin. It is not simply a corroboration of

[10] "A Theological Basis for the World Alliance?" *NRS*, p. 171.
[11] On this subject, cf. Bonhoeffer's critique of Otto Dilschneider's ethics, *Die evangelische Tat* (Gütersloh: Bertelsmann, 1940) in the chapter on "Personal and 'Real' Ethos," *E*, pp. 286–297; and also C, pp. 58 f.; *E*, pp. 205 ff.
[12] Cf. also Bonhoeffer's conversation with Karl Barth in 1941, as reported by Jörgen Glenthøj, "Bonhoeffer und die Ökumene," *MW* II, pp. 116 ff., and the ensuing comment, pp. 198 f. The substance of this doctrine, I would argue, is to be found already in "Thy Kingdom Come," *GS* III, pp. 283 f.

the existing world (*E*, pp. 25 f.).[13] It is important to note that the judgment is not the incarnation itself but the sinlessness of the incarnate One.[14] But it is properly the cross that is the sentence of judgment over the world. "This means in the first place that the whole world has become godless by its rejection of Jesus Christ and that no effort of its own can rid it of this course" (*E*, p. 262).[15] The signature of the world and its reality is henceforth the cross. This means for man, nature, and all the institutions that they have no justification in themselves, that empirical reality is denied and must not be glorified. "But the cross of Christ is the cross of the reconciliation of the world with God, and for this reason the godless world bears at the same time the mark of reconciliation as the free ordinance of God" (*E*, p. 262). This reconciliation is all-embracing. Even this dark and wicked world has been reconciled by Christ. He has conquered it and gathered it under his headship.[16] As the mediator between God and the world "he fills the center of all history"; he is "the secret of the world" (*E*, p. 9).

In the event of incarnation and justification, the reality of God and of the world becomes a unity and a single whole.[17] Here the earlier suggestions of Bonhoeffer—e.g., the whole person, deputyship, etc.,—are given fresh currency, but in a new guise. "The man whom God has taken to himself, sentenced and awakened to new life, this is Jesus Christ. In Him it is all mankind" (*E*, p. 17). Every definition of reality that neglects this truth leads to abstractions. Genuine worldliness for Bonhoeffer means just this: "allowing the whole world to be what it really is before God, namely a world which in its godlessness is reconciled with God" (*E*, p. 263). Just as "the world, the natural, the profane and reason are now all taken up into God from the outset" so, too, all this does not exist for itself. For "that which is Christian is to be found only in that which is of the world, the 'supernatural' only in the natural, the holy only in the profane, and the revela-

[13] Cf. *E*, pp. 292 ff.; pp. 77 ff.; and *GS* III, pp. 458 f.
[14] Cf. *GS* III, p. 234, and Chapter IV, n. 3, above.
[15] Cf. also *E*, p. 189.
[16] Cf. the theology of recapitulation, above.
[17] Cf. also *E*, pp. 88, 61, 67 f., 199.

tional only in the rational" (*E*, pp. 64 f.). This unity is not a static one, conceived only in principle. The worldly is "always seen in the movement of being accepted and becoming accepted by God in Christ" (*E*, p. 65). On the other hand, it does not mean the identity of God and world; unity is "but solely from the reality of Christ, that is to say solely from faith in this ultimate reality" (*E*, p. 65). "In action which is genuinely in accordance with reality there is an indissoluble link between the acknowledgement and the contradiction of the factual. The reason for this is, that reality is first and last not lifeless; but it is the real man, the incarnate God" (*E*, p. 198).

Starting as he does from this dialectical unity between God and the world Bonhoeffer will have no truck with the static dualism of a two-storied universe. He is also at pains to reject several false types of social ethics.

He recognizes that all through church history such two-dimensional thinking has been common. The Middle Ages sought to subject the natural realm to the realm of grace. The "pseudo-Lutheran Christ" of cultural Protestantism exists solely to "sanction the facts as they are" (*E*, p. 199). Among the "enthusiasts," the world was ignored; with a radical eschatology they gave their blessing to every revolution, seeking to build the kingdom of God on earth. The devil cannot be allowed a realm of his own: "The world is not divided between Christ and the devil, but whether it recognizes it or not, it is solely and entirely the world of Christ" (*E*, p. 70). Even a retreat to a monastery or to the inner life is impossible. "In all these schemes the cause of Christ becomes a partial and provincial matter within the limits of reality. It is assumed that there are realities which lie outside the reality that is in Christ. It follows that these realities are accessible by some way of their own, and otherwise than through Christ. However great the importance which is attached to the reality in Christ, it always remains a partial reality amid other realities. The division of the total reality into a sacred and a profane sphere, a Christian and a secular sphere, creates the possibility of existence in a single one of these spheres, a spiritual existence which has no part in secular existence, and a secular existence which can claim autonomy for itself and can exercise this right of autonomy in its dealings with the spiritual sphere" (E, p. 63).[18]

This Christ-reality defines the church's attitude toward the world. The church has no dimension of its own, but "is divided from the world solely by the fact that she affirms in faith the reality of God's acceptance of man, a reality which is the property of the whole world. By allowing this reality to take effect within herself, she testifies that it is effectual for the whole world" (E, p. 72).[19] It has only one word for all and stands as a social community alongside the worldly "estates" under the one dominion of Christ. Not the church but the word of God rules the world (E, p. 265).

4. RESURRECTION AND REALITY

These structures which make up Bonhoeffer's definition of reality must be supplemented briefly in the light of the resurrection. The resurrection shows the conquest of sin and death and the beginnings of new creation. Jesus Christ is the living Lord, to whom "all power is given in heaven and earth" (E, pp. 263 f.). But this does not mean the cessation of all earthly reality. "The night is not yet over but already the dawn is breaking" (E, p. 17). He who knows that the power of death is broken "does not invest earthly things with the title of eternity" (E, p. 17). One does not attempt to build the kingdom of God, but "it is from beyond death that one expects the coming of the new man and of the

---

[18] On the whole subject, cf. GS III, p. 277 ("Thy Kingdom Come"); CD, pp. 40, 137, 234, 239 ff.; GS III, pp. 417 f.; E, pp. 53, 87, 63 f., 223 f. A survey of these initial steps toward a socio-ethical Lutheranism, which Bonhoeffer must have had in mind, is given in Ernst Wolf's "Politica Christi, Das Problem der Sozialethik im Luthertum," Peregrinatio (Munich: Kaiser, [2]1962), pp. 214–228, especially pp. 216–228.

[19] Cf. Bonhoeffer's early statements in CD, pp. 39 ff., 241, 254 f., where he passes a judgment on Luther's return from the monastery into the world similar to that in E, p. 122. At the same time there are other pronouncements in CD, where he stands in danger of seeing things in the way he rejects in E and LPP. Cf., e.g., "Like a sealed train travelling through foreign territory, the Church goes on its way through the world" (CD, p. 251); cf. also CD, pp. 240 f.

new world, from the power by which death had been vanquished" (*E*, p. 17).[20]

5. THE EXTENT OF CHRIST'S DOMINION

(Summary of Sections 1–4)

Thus the dominion of Christ is defined in all-embracing terms. Since he is the Crucified, it is a hidden reign, but nonetheless real for that. There are no "areas of our life" in which we "belong to other lords." [21] "All powers of the world are made subject to Him and must serve Him, each in his own way. The Lordship of Jesus Christ is not the rule of foreign power; it is the Lordship of the Creator, Reconciler and Redeemer" (*E*, p. 264).[22] All things are through him, in him, and unto him. The whole world is "seen, held and freed in this revelation of Christ." [23] This does not mean a Christianizing of the world but, rather, that the worldly orders stand in their worldliness and this-sidedness under the Lordship of Christ.[24] "This, and nothing else, constitutes their 'autonomy.' They are 'autonomous' not in relation to the law of Christ but in relation to earthly heteronomies" (*E*, p. 291), including the church. "Such language cannot be derived from abstract theory or everyday experience, but only by grasping the miracle of the incarnation." [25] Bonhoeffer did not always view the dominion of Christ in this light, as has been shown by the explication of his doctrine of deputyship in Chapter III, section 3, and from various references to *The Cost of Discipleship*. But, in my opinion, it

---

[20] Cf. further the similar discussion in "Thy Kingdom Come" (*GS* III, pp. 276 ff.), and the letter to Theodor Litt (January 22, 1939) in *GS* III, pp. 31–33, especially pp. 32 f.

[21] From the anathema of the Second Confession of Barmen, quoted from A. C. Cochrane, *The Church's Confession under Hitler* (Philadelphia: The Westminster Press, 1962), p. 240.

[22] Cf. also *E*, pp. 287 ff.

[23] J. Moltmann, in *MW* III, p. 49. Cf. also: "Among Christians the whole range of human relationships is embraced by Christ and the Church" (*CD*, p. 230) and, above all, *E*, pp. 55 ff. On the idea of alien dominion, cf. K. Barth, *Church Dogmatics* III/3 (1960), p. 50.

[24] The wording of the above is based on *E*, p. 291.

[25] Quoted from J. Moltmann, above, pp. 62 f.

was precisely in this doctrine that the universality of Christ's dominion was implied from the beginning.

In *Communion of Saints* and *Act and Being*, the world is completely taken up into the dominion of Christ in the church by means of the doctrine of deputyship. The "institutions" are not yet *larvae* of God. This is shown clearly in the lecture "A Theological Basis for the World Alliance?" from which we have already quoted. Here the church is *Christus praesens*, the sole bearer of the commandment (NRS, p. 161). Thus the "order of preservation is to take shape in the preaching activity of the church." Christ's claim to Lordship is extended in this lecture for the first time to include the whole world.[26] "It is not a holy, sacred part of the world which belongs to Christ, but the whole world" (NRS, p. 161). Ernst Wolf asks whether this may not be due to the influence of the social gospel of Bonhoeffer's thought. Bonhoeffer was critical, but not unappreciative, of the social gospel as he had observed it in the United States: "The ruthless seriousness with which the social crisis is exposed and which Christendom summoned to the cause, is the major contribution of American Christianity to the understanding of the Christian message throughout the world" (GS I, p. 110).

In "Thy Kingdom Come" the danger of including the world in a "Christo-monistic system and the danger of an ontological ecclesiasticism" (Ernst Wolf, MW IV, p. 18) appears to be lifting for the first time. Bonhoeffer treats state and church as equal partners. A similar treatment of state and church appears in *Christology* (pp. 65 f.). In an early letter (October 18, 1931) to Helmut Rössler on plans for his trip to India, Bonhoeffer, in a tentative way and still very uncertain of himself, contemplates the possibility of a much wider conception of the dominion of Christ. "One may wonder whether our time is past, and whether the Gospel is given to another nation, perhaps preached in entirely new words and deeds" (GS I, p. 61). *The Cost of Discipleship* marks a certain transition. His doctrine of the ministerial office is changing.[27] The minister is no longer the representative of the church as a *Christus praesens*, but the representative of

---

[26] Ernst Wolf, "Das Letzte und das Vorletzte," MW IV, pp. 17 ff., 23.
[27] Cf. H. C. von Hase, in MW I, p. 44n. and J. Moltmann, above, p. 57.

God toward the congregation (cf. *CS*, pp. 160 ff. and *E*, pp. 258 ff.). This means that the dominion of Christ can be defined in theocratic terms (J. Moltmann, above, pp. 58 f.). And this change can in a way be traced back to *The Cost of Discipleship* (pp. 227 ff.): "The offices of the Church are 'ministries' (διακονίαι, 1 Cor. 12:5). They are appointed in the church of God (1 Cor. 12:28) by Christ (Eph. 4:11) and by the Holy Spirit (Acts 20:28). They are not appointed *by* the church." Although this change in the doctrine of the ministry, which has been pinpointed as a clue to the change in Bonhoeffer's thought generally (H. C. von Hase and J. Moltmann), can likewise be traced back to *The Cost of Discipleship;* yet there *is* a change of orientation in *Ethics* and *Letters and Papers from Prison,* and a widened horizon on the dominion of Christ can be detected. Here is Bonhoeffer's own verdict on the matter: "I thought I could acquire faith by trying to live a holy life, or something like it. It was in this phase that I wrote *The Cost of Discipleship.* To-day I can see the dangers of this book, though I am prepared to stand by what I wrote. Later I discovered and am still discovering up to this very moment that it is only by living completely in this world that one learns to believe" (*LPP*, p. 226). As has been pointed out above, there is nothing for Bonhoeffer, at any rate in *Ethics,* which is not subject to the *regnum Christi.* It cannot be accidental that it is in 1940 that he uses Ephesians 1:10 for the first time, and that the term "genuine worldliness" appears. In the doctrine of the mandates, the church is coordinated with the secular institutions. What seemed to be a certain danger in *Communion of Saints* and *Act and Being,* and right down to *The Cost of Discipleship,* is eliminated in *Ethics:* "The purpose and aim of the dominion of Christ is not to make the worldly order godly or to subordinate it to the Church but to set it free for true worldliness" (*E*, p. 294). The clue to the explanation of this change J. Moltmann (above, p. 56) sees, quite rightly in my opinion, in the following sentence from *Ethics:* "The more exclusively we acknowledge and confess Christ as our Lord, the more fully the wide range of His dominion will be disclosed to us" (*E*, p. 180).[28]

---

[28] Cf. with all this "The Church and the World," *E*, pp. 178–184; "History and Good," *E*, pp. 185 ff. and *GS* III, pp. 455–477, as well as *E*, pp. 101 f.

6. THE "PENULTIMATE"

In Chapter III of *Ethics*, entitled "The Last Things and the Things before Last" (*E*, pp. 79 ff.), Bonhoeffer defines reality in the light of the ultimate as the penultimate.[29] Bonhoeffer finds here an ethical starting point geared to justification, which partially confirms in a new set of terms what has been discussed above.

The justification of the sinner by grace and faith alone is God's final word. "There is nothing that goes beyond a life which is justified by God" (*E*, p. 81). "Justification by grace and faith alone remains in every respect the final word and for this reason, when we speak of the things before last, we must not speak of them as having any value of their own, but we must bring to light their relation to the ultimate" (*E*, p. 84). The relationship between the ultimate and the penultimate is defined in such a way that they are neither in absolute contrast to one another (the radical solution of a thoroughgoing eschatological perspective, i.e., pure otherworldliness; "Thy Kingdom Come" [*GS* III, p. 273], "the Christ of radical enthusiasm" [*E*, p. 199]), nor is there a compromise in which the ultimate is finally eradicated (a doctrine based on creation and preservation, i.e., secularism [*ibid.*], the "pseudo-Lutheran Christ" [*E*, p. 199]) (*E*, pp. 85 ff.). Both positions are contrary to Christ (*E*, pp. 89 f.). "In him alone lies the solution for the problem of the relation between the ultimate and the penultimate. In Jesus Christ we have faith in the incarnate, crucified and risen God. In the incarnation we learn of the love of God for his creation; in the crucifixion we learn of the judgement of God upon all flesh; in the resurrection we learn of God's will for a new world" (*E*, p. 89). In this single, indivisible Christ event the penultimate is neither sanctioned nor destroyed, as has been shown above (*E*, p. 91). "A certain amount of room for the penultimate is left open" (*E*, p. 91). The penultimate precedes and follows the ultimate, it is the "outer covering

[29] Cf. especially Ernst Wolf, in *MW* IV, pp. 17–32, who traces the underlying concern behind this terminology throughout Bonhoeffer's works.

of the ultimate" (*E*, pp. 90, 92). Thus the penultimate is nothing in itself; it cannot justify itself. It only turns into something through the eschatologically ultimate. "The penultimate, then, does not determine the ultimate; it is the ultimate which determines the penultimate" (*E*, pp. 91 f.). That is why the penultimate has to be taken seriously despite its provisional character. In regard to man it means that he must not be robbed of his humanity or be destroyed. For "only man can be justified, precisely because only he who is justified becomes 'man' " (*E*, p. 92). "From this fact follows that it is necessary to see to it that the penultimate, too, is provided with the preaching of the ultimate word of God, lest the destruction of the penultimate should prove a hindrance to the ultimate" (*E*, p. 92). Hence it is important to take care that the word can be heard. This may make it necessary to guard against turning man into an object or a devil. It may mean working to free the slave and to feed the hungry. This does not mean pursuing a program of social reform as such but orienting oneself toward the ultimate. Nor does it deny that "grace must in the end itself prepare and make level its own way" (*E*, p. 94). This is what gives a relative value to such terms as "being human" and "being good," the "natural" (as distinct from creatureliness: "The natural is that which, after the Fall, is directed towards the coming of Christ" [*E*, p. 102]), and justice (*suum cuique*). He who respects penultimate values (e.g., marriage) is still a sinner, "but it still makes a difference whether the penultimate is attended to and taken seriously or not" (*E*, p. 97). The preparation of the way is not the first step to grace. But the penultimate must be respected because it is "preserved and sustained by God for the coming of Christ" (*E*, p. 97).

Here, with a freshly minted terminology unburdened by previous associations, Bonhoeffer picks up again his earlier suggestions about the "order of preservation." [30] It sees all orders as orders of

---

[30] Bonhoeffer was already speaking of the order of preservation at the end of April, 1932 (cf. *GS* I, pp. 121 ff.). There has been some debate as to who first introduced the term, whether Bonhoeffer or Künneth. See J. Glenthøj, in *MW* II, pp. 32 ff. Bonhoeffer continues to use it in his lecture on the World Alliance (*NRS*, pp. 157–172) in his lectures during the winter semester of 1932–1933, *Creation and Fall*. Also to be compared is the "First Draft of the Bethel Confession" (*GS* II, pp. 90 ff.) over which Bonhoeffer exercised a dominant influence; see especially *GS* II, pp. 96–105.

the fallen world; "of no value in themselves, they are accomplished and have purpose only through Christ" (CF, p. 91). "They obtain their value wholly from outside of themselves, from Christ, from the new creation" (NRS, p. 167). They "only exist as long as they are open for the revelation in Christ. Preservation is God's act with the fallen world, through which he guarantees the possibility of a new creation" (NRS, p. 167). Any order must be dissolved "when it closes up itself in itself, grows rigid and no longer permits the proclamation of the revelation" (NRS, p. 167). The church must venture a decision for or against an order of preservation, according as it is open or closed for Christ "in faith in the God who in Christ forgives even the Church its sins" (NRS, p. 167). For Bonhoeffer the condemnation of war and the commandment of international peace are necessary, not as a realization of the gospel, but as a command for "the preservation of the world in the light of Christ" (NRS, p. 168). The new creation, however, is expected from outside.[31]

V.

Man in Christ

It was impossible to write the foregoing chapters without touching again and again on the theme of man in Christ.

In Chapter III, I have shown how Bonhoeffer arrived at the basic term of the person. Man is man only in the continual call of the other who frees him to-be-free-for. This is derived from the God-for-us in Christ. Through the vicarious action of Christ, man is incorporated into the whole person—and thus the new man is

---

[31] On the last paragraph, cf., in addition to J. Glenthøj, op. cit., J. Moltmann, above, pp. 79–81, and Ernst Wolf, in MW IV, pp. 19 f. On the condemnation of war, cf. in addition to the lecture on the World Alliance the lecture at the conference in Gland (August 29, 1932), which belongs to the same period (NRS, pp. 182–189, especially pp. 186 ff.).

possible only within the church: "Man in Christ is man in the church." [1] Bonhoeffer never abandoned this position, thus resisting from the very outset the danger of an "individual ethic." [2]

What I have said in the previous chapter about reality is equally true, *mutatis mutandis*, of man. He, like reality as a whole, knows in the revelatory act of Christ what he is, both as man in Adam and as man in Christ. Only if man recognizes his involvement in the Christ event is it possible to avoid biological and ideological abstractions (*E*, p. 189).[3]

In this dialectic, as we have seen above, man is at once affirmed and negated. God becomes man and intends that we, too, should become men. To despise man (he who despises man despises God), as well as making man a god, is forbidden. "Jesus Christ is not the transfiguration of sublime humanity. He is the 'yes' which God addresses to real man" (*E*, p. 10). We should not extend ourselves above our humanity.[4]

In the cross man sees himself judged and at the same time forgiven and reconciled. The cross reveals to him his sin. He does not come to realize his guilt by self-examination.[5] Because man is in Adam his guilt is infinitely great; he is personally responsible for the sin of all.[6] As an example of Bonhoeffer's recurrence to the "personalism" of his earlier writings, we may quote: "Man is an indivisible whole, not only as an individual in his person and work but also as a member of the community of men and creatures" (*E*, p. 59). But at the same time he knows that he has been accepted by God.

In the resurrection he knows of the end of death and of his own new creation. "Thus man remains man even though he is a new, a risen man, who in no way resembles the old man" (*E*, p. 90).

---

[1] From "Man in Contemporary Philosophy and Theology," inaugural lecture delivered on July 31, 1932 (*NRS*, pp. 50–69). The quotation is from p. 68, corrected.

[2] Cf. *AB*, pp. 123 ff.; *CS*, pp. 216 ff., especially pp. 21 ff.

[3] Cf. also *AB*, pp. 173 ff., especially 45, 79, 91, 190.

[4] Cf. *CD*, pp. 118 f.; *GS* III, p. 232; *E*, pp. 9 ff., 16 f., 21 f.

Cf. the fragment of the theses for the seminar in systematic theology in the summer semester of 1932, "Gibt es eine christliche Ethik?" ("Is There a Christian Ethic?"), *GS* III, pp. 162–165, where he distinguishes between a sinful and a Christian confession of guilt (p. 164); also *E*, pp. 45 f.

[6] Cf. *CS*, pp. 71 f.; *AB*, pp. 162 ff.; *E*, pp. 23 ff., 48 ff.

But until death he remains in the world of the penultimate, yet sees this world in its limited justification.

In the single, indivisible event of the incarnation, cross, and resurrection, man is renewed: "The real, sentenced and renewed man exists nowhere else save in the form of Jesus Christ," (E, pp. 45 f.).

Man is given no rules or norms for his new formation (CD, pp. 162 f.). He "does not take on an independent form of his own, but what gives him form and what maintains him in the new form is always solely the form of Jesus Christ himself" (E, p. 20). "Christ is my life (Phil.1:21)" (E, p. 191). Just like Luther he deems Christ the "persona of the new man." [7] "My life is outside myself, outside the range of my disposal; my life is another than myself; it is Jesus Christ. This is not intended figuratively, as conveying that my life would not be worth living without this other, or that Christ invests my life with a particular quality while allowing it to retain its own independent existence, but my life itself is Jesus Christ" (E, pp. 188 f.). The whole context is worth quoting: "Luther is neither a mystic nor a philosopher of inwardness. But this is what he asserts: 'Faith itself is the subject of Christian action in the world, i.e., Christ himself, who is the persona of the new man.' Instead of the question how to make a man obedient in faith, the question here is where to find the man who is obedient in faith" (E, pp. 188 f.). It is God who accomplishes the change in the form of man "so that man may become, not indeed God, but in the eyes of God, man" (E, p. 20). Man is conformed to Christ and therefore is, in faith, like him. He participates in his suffering, in his vicarious action, by taking upon himself the guilt of others, in the love of God and Christ for the world and man.[8] "Where the I has truly come to the end, truly reaches out of itself, where its grasp is more than a final 'seeking for the self in the self,' there is Christ at work. Hence Luther's countless admonitions not to look on one's own remorse, own faith, but to look on the Lord Jesus himself. While

---

[7] Cited from Ernst Wolf, in EvTh 9 (1949/50), p. 137.

[8] On the fellowship of the cross and on the general affinity between Bonhoeffer's doctrine of the new man and that of Luther, cf. R. Prenter, in MW IV, pp. 33 ff.; see also AB, pp. 160 f., and CD almost throughout.

I am still reflecting on myself in order to find Christ, Christ is not there. If he is really there, I see only him" (*AB*, pp. 160 f.). Thus man is renewed. However, he looks not at himself or at his own good works, but only to Christ.[9]

Another train of thought runs parallel in the Christian's conformity to Christ. This is the theme of the old man and the new, especially in connection with good and evil, a subject of far-reaching importance for ethics. This train of thought is also based on the justification of the sinner, as I will show in greater detail.

Most important, Bonhoeffer describes life in Adam three times as the knowledge of good and evil: in his Barcelona lecture (*NRS*, pp. 39–48), in *Creation and Fall*, and in the section of *Ethics* entitled "The Love of God and the Decay of the World" (*E*, pp. 42 ff.). In contrast to this, life in Christ is the abolition of the knowledge of good and evil.

Man before the fall does not live on his own resources. "Adam's life comes from the middle which is not Adam himself but God. It constantly revolves around this middle" (*CF*, pp. 49 f.). He lives in "unbroken obedience to the Creator" (*CF*, p. 50) because he "does not live in the middle" (*CF*, p. 50). This middle is his limit. "He does not know that the limit can be transgressed—if he did, he would know about evil" (*CF*, p. 52). With this we may compare a passage from the Barcelona lecture: "The original— shall we say childlike—communion between God and man stands beyond this knowledge of good and evil; it knows only of one thing, of the boundless love of God towards man" (*NRS*, p. 41). Disobeying the command, he eats from the tree of knowledge of good and evil. In consequence, man now stands in the middle and has lost the limit which had circumscribed his life. He is now left to his own resources, he is "like God." He is his own creator. He knows himself to be the origin of his life. He can no longer live before God, yet he must live and is thus dead. He is schizophrenic man, man in ethical conflict, torn apart, the Pharisee (*E*, p. 51): "The Pharisee is not an adventitious historical phenomenon of a particular time. He is the man to whom only the knowledge of good and evil has come to be of importance in his entire life; in other words he is simply the man of disunion." For

[9] Cf. also *E*, p. 80.

Bonhoeffer, "Man's shame is his reluctant acknowledgment of revelation, of the other person, of God" (*E*, p. 80). "Instead of seeing God, man sees himself. . . . He perceives that he is naked" (*E*, p. 145). In addition to shame, the consequence of the fall is the development of conscience. "In shame man is reminded of his disunion with God and with other men; conscience is the sign of man's disunion with himself. Conscience is farther from the origin than shame; . . . it is the voice of the apostate life which desires at least to remain one with itself. It is the call of the unity of man with himself. . . . For conscience life falls into two parts; what is permitted and what is forbidden. There is no positive commandment" (*E*, p. 148). Having become his own judge man also becomes his own creator. His relationship to God, and therefore to others, is reversed (*E*, p. 143). "Conscience pretends to be the voice of God and the standard for the relation of other men. It is therefore from his right relation to himself that man is to recover the right relation to God and to other men. This reversal is the claim of the man who has become like God in his knowledge of good and evil. Man has become the origin of good and evil. He does not deny his evil; but in conscience man summons himself, who has become evil, back to his proper, better self, to good" (*E*, p. 149). The ethic of fallen man is aimed at overcoming the division, it is a casuistic ethic of duty, a way of man to God.[10] It "leads only to still greater disunion and to persistence in the defection from the origin" (*E*, p. 155).

What is needed now is for man to find his way back from being like God to creatureliness. He must recover his center, limit, and origin. Christ is the new center, this cessation of the knowledge of good and evil. "Jesus Christ lives for him and in him and . . . occupies within him exactly the space which was previously occupied by his own knowledge of good and evil" (*E*, p. 165), and is thus his *persona*. It appears as though Bonhoeffer is here making important deductions from creation. Actually, however, they are derived from Christology, as I will try to show in the following excursus.[11]

[10] Cf. also Karl Barth, *Church Dogmatics* III/4 (1961), p. 10.
[11] Cf., also, above, Chapter III, sections 1 and 3.

EXCURSUS

In *Creation and Fall*, Bonhoeffer points out more than once that the creation should be viewed only in the light of Christ (cf. especially *CF*, pp. 7 f.). He expresses it most clearly in pages 56–57 of *Creation and Fall*: "But as those who only live and have a history through Christ, our imagination cannot help us to know about the beginning. We can only know about it from the middle, from Christ, as those who are freed in faith from the knowledge of good and evil and from death, and who can make Adam's picture their own only faith." [12] Thus the knowledge of good and evil cannot include knowledge of man's fall from his origin. "It is true that the Pharisee is seen in this light only from the standpoint of unity already recovered, from the standpoint of Jesus. The Pharisee himself can know himself only in his virtues and vices, but not in his essence, in his apostasy from the origin" (*E*, p. 156).[13] This proves that for Bonhoeffer every statement about the old man and the new are derived exclusively from Christology.

The statement that Christ now occupies exactly the place previously occupied by the knowledge of good and evil is confirmed by another statement about the conscience. Conscience remains in a formal way. But emancipated as it now is in Jesus Christ it calls man to unity with his regained center, Jesus Christ, and acquires a new content: "Jesus Christ has become my conscience. This means that I can now find unity with myself only in the surrender of my ego to God and to men. The origin and goal of my conscience is not a law but it is the living God and the living man as he confronts me in Jesus Christ" (*E*, pp. 212 f.). This is an exact parallel, though only a formal one, to the statement: "When the national socialist says 'my conscience is Adolf Hitler' that, too, is an attempt to find a foundation for the unity of his own ego somewhere beyond himself" (*E*, p. 121). The

[12] Cf. also *CF*, pp. 74 f.
[13] Cf. above, Chapter V, n. 5.

ethical conflict has thus been lifted. Man is no longer autonomous; he stands as man justified, in singleminded obedience toward his Lord, who as the new center of his existence is his life. He has been freed for action in love and free responsibility. His own good has been hidden from him. Good is only the will of God; he is only called upon to do it. Hearing and action form a unity.[14] The concept of the center is of crucial importance for Bonhoeffer's theology. The above has dealt with the center lost after the fall and with Jesus as the new center of existence. In *Creation and Fall*, Bonhoeffer mentions that the cross is the new center of the world (*CF*, pp. 95 f.). In *Christology* he designates Christ as the center of human existence and as the Mediator between God and nature (*C*, pp. 61–67). In *The Cost of Discipleship* there is for the Christian no direct relationship between himself and God, between any other things in this world and men, even between husband and wife in marriage. Christ is always the center and the Mediator.[15]

For further christological deductions and for the elimination of any possible psychological misunderstandings, the following quotation will suffice: "By virtue of his incarnation he has come between man and his natural life. There can be no turning back, for Christ bars the way. By calling us he has cut us off from all immediacy with the things of this world" (*CD*, p. 85). The fact "that Christ is the centre of our existence does not mean that he is the centre of our personality, our thought and our feeling. Christ is the centre even when he stands on the periphery of our consciousness. . . . The character of the statement about his centrality is not psychological, but ontological-theological. It does not relate to our personality, but to our being a person before God. The centre of the person is not demonstrable" (*C*, p. 62). Thus Christ is the center who is the object of faith. We may also compare Bonhoeffer's observation on the sinlessness of Jesus and his incognito existence: because he really is the likeness of flesh, his sinlessness is only a matter of faith, not a demonstrable fact (*C*, p. 113). Similarly, there is his attempt to avert any miscon-

---

[14] For singleminded obedience, cf. especially *CD*, pp. 69 ff.; also *E*, pp. 158 ff., 5 ff. On the psychological misinterpretation see following paragraph.
[15] Cf. especially *C*, pp. 84–91, 147; *E*, pp. 190 f.

ception about the cessation of the knowledge of good and evil, singleminded obedience, etc. as though they were "psychologically observable data" (*E*, p. 160).[16]

The new life is no empty dream. Bonhoeffer says as much in *Ethics* (p. 80): "In Christ all this is truth and reality, and just because it is not a dream the life of the man who experiences the presence of Christ is henceforward no longer a lost life, but it has become a justified life, a life justified by grace alone." The concept of the center is equally important for the nonreligious interpretation.[17]

Before I embark on the important consequences of all this for ethics let me take conscience as an illustration of how the relationship, for Bonhoeffer, of life in Adam and life in Christ is apparent in the new man. As has already been mentioned above, conscience remains in a formal sense and calls for unity with Jesus Christ. But man still lives in the penultimate. His life in Adam may be weakened in Christ, but it is not completely subdued.[18] Conscience is still what it always was: an appeal not only for unity with the new center but also for unity with oneself. Thus, when believers take upon themselves the guilt of others, it acts as a corrective. For "conscience . . . contains fundamental features of the law of life" (*E*, p. 216). Not everyone can accept the same responsibility. "There are responsibilities which I cannot carry without breaking down under their weight" (*E*, p. 215). Strength to carry responsibility can grow and will grow, "yet in the concrete instance the summons of conscience to unity with oneself in Jesus Christ remains irresistible, and it is this which explains the infinite multiplicity of responsible decisions" (*E*, p. 215). Vicarious action steers between setting up one's own ego as an absolute and setting up the other man as an absolute (*E*, p. 196). This, however, is said only to prevent misuse, for it is no

[16] With this may also be compared *CD*, p. 206, n. 1, and J. Moltmann, above, p. 28.

[17] Cf. especially *LPP*, p. 191, in the letter of May 25, 1944, and *LPP*, pp. 161–166, in the letter of April 30, 1944, as well for his suggestion that the commandment implies permission (cf. below, Chapter VI, section 3). In this connection the section in *Ethics* entitled "Christ, and Good People" (*E*, p. 181) should be consulted. And on the subject as a whole, cf. especially R. Prenter, in *MW* IV, pp. 40 ff.

[18] Cf. especially *CS*, p. 71.

longer conscience which is the ultimate, but fellowship with Jesus Christ. Thus Bonhoeffer is able to say: "But the law is no longer the last thing; there is still Jesus Christ; for that reason, in the contest between conscience and concrete responsibility, the free decision must be given for Christ" (E, p. 216). It is precisely in taking upon oneself the guilt of others that conscience shows its purity (E, pp. 212 ff.).

Jesus Christ is the center of the new humanity transcending the knowledge of good and evil. The consequence of this is "that the question of good can find its answer only in Christ" (E, p. 56).[19] Everyone who seeks to deal with Christian ethics must endure the accusation: "The two questions which alone impel him to concern himself with the problem of ethics, 'How can I be good?' and 'How can I do good?' and instead of these he must ask the utterly and totally different question 'What is the will of God?' This requirement is so immensely far-reaching because it presupposes a decision with regard to the ultimate reality; it presupposes a decision of faith. If the ethical problem presents itself essentially in the form of enquiries about one's own being good and doing good, this means that it has already been decided that it is the self and the world which are the ultimate reality. The aim of all ethical reflection is, then, that I myself shall be good and that the world shall become good through my action" (E, p. 55). Or again: "The knowledge of good and evil seems to be the aim of all ethical reflection. The first task of Christian ethics is to invalidate this knowledge" (E, p. 142).

Thus ethics, as a way from man to God, is absolutely ruled out. For the way of God to man is the way of grace, the way of love in Christ (NRS, pp. 40 f.). The will of God has to be followed in concrete situations. Consequently there are no principles involved. Hence, in his Barcelona lecture Bonhoeffer can say with some ex-aggeration: "There are no actions which are bad in themselves— even murder can be justified—there is only faithfulness to God's will or deviation from it" (NRS, pp. 44 f.). The deed then is not justified from any principle, a law or an idea. Judgment is left to God's grace. This conclusion may be supported from the following passage: "When the deed is performed with the responsible

[19] Cf. Karl Barth, Church Dogmatics II/2 (1957), p. 548.

weighing up of all the personal and objective circumstances and in the awareness that God has become *man* and that it is *God* who has become man, then this deed is delivered up solely to God at the moment of its performance. Ultimate ignorance of one's own good and evil, and with it a complete reliance upon grace, is an essential property of responsible historical action. The man who acts ideologically sees himself justified in his idea; the responsible man commits his action into the hands of God and lives by God's grace and favour." [20] It is in the light of recovered unity, of justification and reconciliation, that Christian ethics can say: "What is of ultimate importance is now no longer that I should become good, or that the condition of the world should be made better by my action, but [the fact] that the reality of God should show itself everywhere should be the ultimate reality" (*E*, p. 55). The question of the good can find its answer only in Christ (*E*, p. 56).[21]

VI.

The Commandment

Bonhoeffer was constantly concerned with the question of commandment and righteous action. What is the source of the commandment, which not only consists in general principles, universally true, but is valid for us today, here and now? Who has authority to talk like that? From what has been said thus far it should be clear that our answer must be related both to the reality of our environment and with Christ, who entered into his reality, judging it and reconciling it and gathering all created things under himself as Head.

[20] *E*, pp. 303 f.; cf. also *E*, pp. 165 f., 203 f.; GS III, p. 461, etc.
[21] For Karl Barth cf.: "The good of human action consists in the fact that it is determined by the divine command" (*Church Dogmatics* II/2 [1957], p. 547).

1. NO "ORDER OF CREATION"

Creation is fallen and silent; "The continuity of Word and nature has been lost" (C, p. 54). The entering of Christ into reality means the judgment as well as affirmation of creation. It certainly does not mean "investing the established order with a halo of spirituality" (CD, p. 234). It is not the world that has accepted God, but God who has accepted the world. Thus Bonhoeffer argues: "The commandment of God does not spring from the created world. It comes down from above" (E, p. 246). This is why as early as 1932 he rejected a theology based on the order of creation.[1] On the one hand, with the help of "unbroken orders of creation" the possibility is opened up for man to return into a sinless world, thereby making Christ's death upon the cross superfluous (GS II, p. 100).[2] On the other hand, everything can be justified, e.g., war or the class struggle which only have to be decreed to be God-given (NRS, pp. 169 f.). But the commandment exists only in Christ. In the world there are no longer any direct relationships. Or, to quote another passage of similar import: "It is a theological error of the first magnitude to exploit the doctrine of Christ the Mediator so as to justify direct relationships with the things of this world. It is sometimes argued that if Christ is the Mediator he has borne all sin which underlies our direct relationships with the world and that he justifies us in them. Jesus has reconciled us to God; we can, it is supposed, return to the world and enjoy our direct relation with it with a good conscience— although that world is the very world which crucified Christ! This is to equate the love of God with the love of the world" (CD, p. 87). This is what Bonhoeffer calls cheap grace. He will have no truck with the "pseudo-Lutheran Christ who exists solely for the purpose of sanctioning facts" (E, p. 199). This is equally important for the doctrine of vocation. Every place as well as every situation is qualified only by the call of Jesus Christ. The call

[1] Cf. NRS, pp. 157–173, 179–182; GS II, 96 ff. On these passages see above, Chapter IV, section 6.
[2] "First Draft of the Bethel Confession" (GS II, pp. 90 ff.).

to discipleship does not sanction the "vocation": "We have by now made it clear that for the Christian a life within the terms of a secular calling has a definite limit. It may well happen that after we have been called to a secular profession we shall be called upon to quit it. This of course is to be understood in the way both St. Paul and Luther understood it" (*CD*, p. 239).[3]

This rejection of the order of creation has equally important consequences for Bonhoeffer's views on the Jewish question. "If the Holy Ghost has spoken and we listen instead to the call of blood and nature, or to our personal sympathies or antipathies, we are profaning the sacrament" (*CD*, p. 230). How the "orders" are integrated into the dominion of Christ is shown by his doctrine of the mandates (see below, pp. 139–149).

2. THE COMMANDMENT AND THE ETHICAL DIRECTIONS OF THE BIBLE

It would be tempting for a Protestant theology based on the Bible simply to accept the commandment of God and the biblical directions "as it is explained in the decalogue, in the sermon on the mount and in the apostolic paranesis" (*E*, p. 216), and as it is condensed in the double commandment of love for God and neighbor. Already in his Barcelona lecture Bonhoeffer rejects the legalistic approach to the biblical directions, including the commandment of love as the basis for Christian ethics. This understanding pervades his whole work.[4] Let me quote from the Barcelona lecture: "The commandment of love is not exclusively Christian, but was already generally recognised and widespread at the time of Jesus" (*NRS*, p. 42). Again, "It is the greatest of misunderstandings to make the commandments of the Sermon on the Mount into laws once again by referring them literally to the present. This is not only senseless, because it is impracticable, but still more, it is against the spirit of Christ, who brought freedom

---

[3] On the doctrine of vocation, cf. *E*, pp. 229 ff., and also the doctrine of the mandates.
[4] For the early Bonhoeffer, the most important passages are: *NRS*, pp. 42 f., 45 f., 162. For Karl Barth, cf. *Church Dogmatics* III/4 (1961), p. 12.

from the law. The whole life, say, of Count Tolstoy and so many others has been lived under this misunderstanding. There are no ethical directions in the New Testament which we should have, or even could have, taken over literally" (NRS, p. 45).

Despite this, Bonhoeffer was inclined to attach undue importance to the Sermon on the Mount, as may be seen from his letter to Erwin Sutz, dated February 28, 1934 (GS I, pp. 40 f.) and from that to his family, dated January 1, 1935 (GS III, pp. 24 f.). As for the legalistic understanding of the Sermon on the Mount, it still remains to be asked: "Whence does the Church know God's commandment for the moment?" (NRS, p. 165). Christ did not enter into a general principle or commandment, but into the concrete history of humanity. Hence his commandment must always be concrete and situational.

The legalistic, abstract understanding of the Sermon on the Mount "is preached as the law of all secular action. It takes the place of state laws" (GS III, p. 471).[5] The collapse of the program of the enthusiasts leads to the Sermon on the Mount's being treated as a private ethic, the "Ethic of Jesus." Here no attempt is made to apply it to history.[6] But Bonhoeffer cannot leave the Sermon on the Mount to only one of the two spheres which are reconciled in Christ. He finds a key to the exegesis of the Sermon on the Mount by refusing to separate the commandment from its author.[7]

It is the exposition of the existence of him in whom God and the world are reconciled, in whom justification occurred. Thus it is Christ, "who alone has borne and experienced the essence of the real in His own body, who has spoken from the standpoint of reality as no man on earth can do" (E, p. 199). As the word

[5] From "Die Geschichte und das Gute" ("History and the Good"), GS III, pp. 455–477. Bonhoeffer did not think this treatment sufficiently explicit, but it does agree with E, pp. 185–216. As far as our present theme is concerned, however, the treatment is more detailed than in the chapter in Ethics. That is the main reason why most of our quotations are taken from it. On the Sermon on the Mount cf. especially the agreement of GS III, pp. 465, 470 f., with E, pp. 199 ff.
[6] Cf. GS III, pp. 464 f.; E, pp. 186 f., 288 f., etc.
[7] Cf. especially the exposition of the Sermon on the Mount in CD, pp. 93–198, and in E, pp. 154–178.

of him who justifies, the Sermon on the Mount frees "man's vision, distorted as it is and led astray by self-love to the clear knowledge of reality, of the neighbor and of the world, thus, and only thus, making him ready to see where real responsibility lies" (*GS* III, p. 476). Thus he is freed to love the other man, freed for responsible, Christlike action. So the Sermon on the Mount is of universal application, "and can in no wise be restricted to an isolated religious sphere" (*GS* III, p. 473). It is applicable even to political action. "It is never the task of the Church to preach the natural instinct of self-preservation to the state" (*E*, p. 323), yet even power can be used as an expression of the love of God.[8]

Bonhoeffer is close to Luther on this point, as Ernst Wolf has observed: "The much debated and frequently misinterpreted distinction of the spiritual and secular realms may not be interpreted as far as Luther is concerned as though the former were an expression of the goodness of God, the latter of his power. *Both* of them are an expression of the love which is shown to men by God." [9] The same is true of the apostolic parenesis and even of the Decalogue. All biblical directions are commandments of the living God: "The decalogue and the Sermon on the Mount are not, therefore, two different ethical ideals, but one single call to concrete obedience towards the God and Father of Jesus Christ" (*E*, p. 323).[10]

3. THE COMMANDMENT AS PERMISSION

The commandment of God is always a commandment revealed in Jesus Christ (*E*, pp. 245 f.). Only from him "who brings and promises the new world" (*NRS*, p. 166) can it come. This Jesus Christ is the reconciliation of the reality of God and of the world. He is the center of man, nature, and history. It is he who assumed full humanity and emancipated mankind from its ethical conflict.

[8] Cf. *E*, pp. 295 f., and *GS* III, p. 477.
[9] Ernst Wolf, *Peregrinatio*, pp. 233 f.
[10] From "On the Possibility of the Word of the Church to the World," Part II, IV of *Ethics* (*E*, pp. 318–325, undoubtedly from the Tegel period).

That explains why Bonhoeffer does not take the commandment as an ethical border event or as "summary of all ethical propositions" (*E*, p. 244). If it were so it would be once more within man's own capabilities. Rather, it is permission,[11] freedom.[12] "God gives before He demands" (*E*, p. 108).[13]

The ethical watches over "the untransgressable frontier of life" (*E*, p. 247) and enjoys its rights for a certain period. In biblical terms it is the law (*E*, p. 253). "God's commandment, revealed in Jesus Christ, embraces the whole of life. It does not only, like the ethical, keep watch on the untransgressable frontier of life, but it is at the same time the centre and fullness of life" (*E*, p. 247). "The boundary arises from the centre and the fullness of life with the commandment of God; it is not the other way round" (*E*, p. 252). Here we come once more upon the important term "center." [14] This center is the incarnate God; Christ has entered the whole of life. This is to be explained from Bonhoeffer's Christology, not from a doctrine of vitalism.[15]

Bonhoeffer is entirely aware that the commandment includes the ethical and that it sets free as well as binds (*E*, p. 242). Yet he can say: "The commandment of God permits man to be man before God. It allows the flood of life to flow freely. It lets man eat, drink, sleep, work, rest and play. It does not interrupt him. It does not continually ask him whether he ought to be sleeping, eating, working or playing, or whether he has some more urgent duties" (*E*, p. 250). The commandments are kept because they are accepted voluntarily. Man achieves wholeness not as a "student of ethics" (*E*, p. 249) but rather as the one who also knows about

---

[11] Cf. *CD*, p. 199; *E*, pp. 258 ff., 253.

[12] Permission is not an *adiaphoron*, an indifferent matter. Bonhoeffer agrees with Kant and Fichte when they condemn the term "the permitted." But Bonhoeffer contrasts permission with the idealistic concept of duty (*E*, pp. 238 ff.).

[13] On "privilege," cf. Ernst Wolf, in MW IV, p. 31: "The question arises . . . whether the language of questionable privileges was a felicitous choice. Karl Barth prefers to speak of 'freedom to live.' "

[14] Cf. above, Chapter V, especially n. 14.

[15] Cf. Jürgen Moltmann, in MW III, p. 53, n. 6: "Just as in the early Barth we find neo-Kantian forms of thought, Bonhoeffer's terminology is close to the so-called 'philosophy of life' whose protagonists include Dilthey, Nietzsche, Tönnies, Ortega y Gasset, etc. Cf. O. F. Bollnow, *Die Lebensphilosophie* (1958)."

the "sphere of freedom" (*LPP*, p. 124). So the commandment leads away from the ethic of duty by enjoining freedom.[16]

In *Letters and Papers from Prison* this comes out even more strongly and is equally based on "the revelation of God in Christ" who is "the centre of life" (*LPP*, p. 191). The Christian does not diminish his humanity by tempering his passions (John the Baptist the ascetic *versus* Jesus the utterly human—passages like Mark 1:6, Matt. 9:14 f.; 11:18, and others have something to say here). He is as completely human as Jesus was. The Old Testament, which acquired increasing importance for Bonhoeffer during the period of his Tegel imprisonment, is as it were a series of examples of what it means to be a whole man. The participation of the Christian in Christ consists in tasting joy and sorrow to the full. "Pain and joy are also part of the polyphony of life" (*LPP*, p. 177). From this he draws the conclusion: "The Christian, unlike the devotees of the salvation myths, does not need a last refuge in the eternal from earthly tasks and difficulties. But like Christ himself ('My God, my God, why hast thou forsaken me?') he must drink the earthly cup to the lees, and only in his doing that is the crucified and risen Lord with him, and he crucified and risen with Christ. This world must not be prematurely written off" (*LPP*, pp. 205 f.).[17]

4. THE DOCTRINE OF THE MANDATES

A life under the commandment of God takes place in the context of the mandates, according to Bonhoeffer. The mandates are subject to the dominion of Christ within the limits set by the Decalogue. Bonhoeffer later abandons the term used in 1932–1933 for "order of creation," [18] viz., "order of preserva-

---

[16] On all this, cf. further *E*, pp. 145 f.; also the section entitled "The Natural," pp. 101 ff., especially pp. 113 ff., on the purpose and joy of bodily existence.
[17] From the same work, cf. especially the following passages: *LPP*, pp. 103 f., 113, 122 ff., 175 ff., 189 ff., 204 ff. And on the same subject, cf. also Hannelis Schulte, "In den Tatsachen selbst ist Gott" (on the significance of the Old Testament for Christian preaching in the last letters of Dietrich Bonhoeffer), *EvTh* 22 (1962), pp. 441–448.
[18] Cf. above, Chapter VI, section 1.

tion," [19] because of the misunderstanding it led to during the church struggle. In his lecture on the World Alliance he was still treating the whole church as *Christus praesens*, authorized to keep the commandments. But by the end of the year, in "Thy Kingdom Come" as well as in his Christology lectures, he was placing the state as an "order" alongside the church as "miracle." In the combination of "the breaking through of all the orders" with the "ordinances as preservation, waiting for the miracle" (*GS* III, p. 279), the kingdom of God exists in the penultimate under the twin institutions of church and state (*GS* III, p. 282). Let me quote from the lecture on Christology: "Christ is present to us in a double form, as church and as state. . . . The state is the rule of God 'with his left hand' (Luther, WA 36, 385, 6–9; WA 52, 26, 20–26). As long as Christ was on earth he was the rule of God. When he was crucified, the rule broke in two, one by his right hand and one by the left hand of God. Now his rule can be known only as twofold, as church and as state." (*C*, p. 66). "In the genuine relation and limitation of both the kingdom of God is a reality" (*C*, p. 283). On the ground of the universal dominion of Christ, and as a visible phenomenon within the world, the mandates become in *Ethics* the bearer of the commandment. "That is, for Bonhoeffer, this distinctive freedom, to affirm 'the polyphony of life' (*LPP*, p. 175), the thing that makes possible 'the many different dimensions of life' (*LPP*, p. 189), springs from faith in the prevailing, latent and eschatological unity of all things in Christ." [20]

The Basis for the Mandates. Bonhoeffer makes two starts in his *Ethics* on the doctrine of mandates. In *Ethics*, pages 73–78, he begins with the christological unity of God and the world and in *Ethics*, pages 252–258, with the authorization conferred by the commandment. He generally speaks of four mandates: labor (culture), marriage and the family, government (state), and church. In *Ethics*, page 252, he substitutes "culture" for "labor." According to *Ethics*, page 73, labor is an aspect of culture. In *Letters and Papers from Prison*

[19] Cf. above, Chapter IV, section 6 and n. 30.
[20] J. Moltmann, in MW III, p. 64.

(pp. 124 ff.), culture and education, of which friendship is one aspect, are not classified under the mandate of labor ("the sphere of freedom"), but under the church. As far as I can discover, Bonhoeffer never speaks of five mandates, but invariably of only four.[21] With this "doctrine drawn from the Bible" he seeks to replace the Lutheran doctrine of the three estates, *oeconomicus, politicus* and *hierarchicus*" (E, p. 294). "For lack of a better word" he employs the term "mandate" as a substitute for the misleading terms, "institution, estate and office" (E, p. 254).

All reality is created by and for Christ. Christ entered into it, judging and reconciling it and uniting it under his own headship. Thus the world, whether it knows it or not, stands in a relationship to Christ: "This relativeness of the world to Christ assumes concrete form in certain mandates of God in the world" (E, p. 73). The choice of the term "mandate" instead of "order" expresses their character as divine institutions rather than self-determined entities. For labor, marriage, etc., are not self-subsistent, empirical data: they owe their existence to their relationship to Christ. It is because they are commanded that they are divine, not because they *exist*. "They are introduced into the world from above as orders or 'institutions' of the reality of Christ, that is to say, of the reality of the love of God for the world and for men which is revealed in Jesus Christ. This means that they are not in any sense products of history" (E, p. 255). In them "the conferment of divine authority on an earthly agent takes place (E, p. 254). It is not that the mandates are having an intrinsic value of their own. Only "through the divine mandate what has concrete being acquires a relative justification" (E, p. 74). Mandate is the "legitimization" of "divine authority on an earthly agent" (E, p. 254). "These institutions are therefore not a second divine authority, side by side with the God of Jesus Christ; but they are the place at which the God of Jesus Christ secures obedience to Himself" (E, p. 322). This point is of major importance for the whole of Bonhoeffer's theology, and can be substantiated from

[21] *Contra* J. Moltmann, in MW III, p. 62, and K. Barth, *Church Dogmatics*, III/4 (1961), pp. 21 f.

many passages in *The Cost of Discipleship* and *Ethics.*[22] Here is
an additional passage: "The calling in the New Testament sense
is never a sanctioning of worldly institutions as such; its 'yes' to
them always includes at the same time an extremely emphatic
'no,' an extremely sharp protest against the world. . . . Now a
man takes up his position against the world *in* the world; the
calling is the place at which the call of God is answered, the place
at which man lives responsibly" (*E*, p. 223).

The extent of Bonhoeffer's agreement on this point with Karl
Barth is shown by the following quotation from *Church Dogmatics:* "They are the sphere in which God commands and man
is obedient, but not laws according to which God commands and
man does right or wrong. . . . Thus the emergence of these
spheres, relationships or orders does not make possible a return
to casuistry. They are not universal ethical truths, but only the
general form of the one supremely particular truth of the ethical
event which is inaccessible as such to the casuistical grasp." [23]

The Coordination of the Mandates. "The Mandates are dependent *solely* on the commandment of God" (*E*, pp. 254 f.). They ac-
complish their task only perfectly by being "limited first by God,
who confers the commission" ("the dominion of Christ . . . over
them" [*E*, p. 295]) and "in conjunction, in combination and in
opposition" (*E*, p. 257). "No single one of these mandates is
sufficient in itself or can claim to replace all the others" (*E*, p.
257). Each mandate is, as it were, answerable to God alone.[24]
All men are subject to all four of the mandates. "This means that
there can be no retreating from a 'secular' into a 'spiritual' sphere.
There can be only the practice, the learning of the Christian life
under these four mandates of God" (*E*, p. 73). Every man obeys
God in each of the mandates. The church can no more claim to
dominate the world than the state can claim to be "omnipo-
tent." [25] In this complex situation the mandates serve "to confront man with the one and entire reality which is manifested to

---

[22] Cf. above, Chapter VI, section 1 and n. 3.
[23] Karl Barth, *Church Dogmatics* III/4 (1961), pp. 29 f.
[24] See J. Moltmann, above p. 86.
[25] From "Gedanken zu William Paton: The Church and the New Order"
(*GS* I, p. 358).

us in Jesus Christ. Thus here again all lines converge in the reality of the body of Jesus Christ, in which God and man become one (*E*, p. 77).[26]

The Bearers of the Mandates as Deputies. As deputies of God, the bearers of the mandates are authorized to engage in ethical discourse. This is based on the fact that the commandment comes down from above. This vertical relationship plays a major role in Bonhoeffer's thinking, not least in the doctrine of the mandates and of the authorization of the bearers of the mandates. It is based on the condescension of God in Christ and on the vicarious action of Christ. "The bearers of the mandates do not receive their commission from below; their task is not to expound and execute desires of the human will, but in a strict and unaltera-ble sense they hold their commission from God, they are deputies and representatives of God" (*E*, p. 255). They are antitype of the dominion of Christ on earth.[27] "Because He is life all life is determined by Him to be deputyship" (*E*, p. 195). Father, states-man, and teacher—all act in deputyship.[28] "The father acts for the children, working for them, caring for them, interceding, fight-ing and suffering for them. Thus in a real sense he is their deputy. He is not an isolated individual, but he combines in himself the selves of a number of human beings" (*E*, p. 194). This opens up new applications for those christological structures of deputyship derived from *Communion of Saints*, viz., social relationships and "being for others."

It has rightly been pointed out [29] that in Bonhoeffer this thought of "from above downward" is already adumbrated in his radio address of March, 1933.[30] Two passages will illustrate this:

---

[26] Bonhoeffer sees the decisive feature of Luther's teaching of the three in-stitutions, or powers, in their coordination rather than in their organization in a hierarchical structure. Cf. *E*, pp. 296 f., and *C*, p. 283 (quoted above, p. 140). Ernst Wolf reaches the same conclusion in *Peregrinatio*, pp. 214 ff., especially pp. 232 ff. The reader will find further bibliography there. Cf. also J. Moltmann, above, pp. 71 ff.

[27] Cf. especially *E*, pp. 219 f., 81 f.

[28] Cf. also the shift in Bonhoeffer's doctrine of the ministerial office.

[29] G. Meuss, "Bericht über die 3. Tagung zum Studium von Bonhoeffer's Werk," *MW* III, p. 9.

[30] "The Leader and the Individual in the Younger Generation," *NRS*, pp. 190–204.

" 'The authority of the leader or the authority of an office?' And here we have reached the burning question of the present day. The leader has authority from below, from those whom he leads, while the office has authority from above" (NRS, p. 200). "Thus the Leader points to the office, but Leader and office point to the final authority itself, before which Reich or state are penultimate authorities. Leaders or offices which set themselves up as gods mock God and the individual who stands alone before him, and must perish. Only the Leader who himself serves the penultimate and the ultimate authority can find faithfulness" (NRS, p. 204).

The Individual Mandates. The task and basis of the mandates in relation to Christ are specifically as follows:

Labor is supra-lapsarian, and even after the fall still has the mission of participating creatively in "the glorification and service of Jesus Christ" (E, p. 74). "Through the divine mandate of labor there is to come into being a world which, knowingly or not, is waiting for Christ, designed for Christ, open to Christ, serves Him and glorifies Him" (E, p. 75). It also brings into being an antitype of the world to come. Thus labor has a mission in the realm of the penultimate, preparing the way for the ultimate, the entrance of Christ.

Marriage is equally supra-lapsarian. "Through marriage men are brought into being for the glorification and the service of Jesus Christ" (E, p. 75). Parents exist to educate their children in obedience to Christ. Marriage represents the relationship between Christ and the church.[31]

Government has its archetype in the theocracy of Christ and presupposes the mandates of labor and marriage. Bonhoeffer prefers to speak of government rather than of the state, because it expresses more clearly its commission from above. The relatively best form of government in his opinion is "a properly understood divine right of government" (E, p. 316). I hope to have shown that this has in the last analysis a christological basis and is only to a secondary degree explicable from Bonhoeffer's bourgeois conservatism. The radio lecture might provide a clue to this

---

[31] Cf. CF, pp. 61 f.; E, pp. 308 f. For Karl Barth, cf. *Church Dogmatics* III/3 (1960), p. 49.

seemingly anachronistic opinion. Hitler was for him the negative example of a "leader" who came to power from below. Any attempt to justify government from natural law or from the fall (preservation), Bonhoeffer rejects. Government, like everything else in the created world, is grounded in Christ. It is he who maintains it and furnishes its goals.[32] Government is uncreative, and must never take the initiative in affairs of labor, science, or culture. Nor does it institute marriage. "Government maintains created things in their proper order" (*E*, p. 308). By the establishment of law and by force of the sword the governing authority preserves the world for the reality of Jesus Christ" (*E*, p. 76). Government, "independent of the religious decision" (*E*, p. 312), has its genuine worldliness when it regards itself as limited by the other mandates, respecting them and fulfilling its own task faithfully. It will not, for instance, take over the propagation of the gospel. Government is not "a secondary authority, side by side with authority of Christ, but its own authority is only a form of the authority of Christ. In his obedience to government the Christian is obedient to Christ (*E*, p. 311).[33] Thus government is the servant of Christ and in this way has a task in the sphere of the penultimate.[34]

The *church's* mission is to proclaim Christ incarnate, crucified, and exalted "as the Lord and Saviour of the world" (*E*, p. 261). This mandate "is concerned therefore, with the eternal salvation of the whole world" (*E*, p. 76). The church has only one word and one commandment for believers and unbelievers alike. To the world it proclaims reality as it is in Christ,[35] thus setting it free

[32] See especially Appendix III of *Ethics*, "State and Church" (*E*, pp. 297–317), where he discusses the various forms of government, especially *E*, pp. 297–303, 316 f.
[33] Cf. above, Chapter VI, section 2 and n. 8.
[34] Cf. with the whole chapter of government and certain aspects of the doctrine of the mandates, especially "Thy Kingdom Come"; "The Church and the Jewish Question" (1933), *NRS*, pp. 221–229; Appendix III of *Ethics* (pp. 297–317), "State and Church" (1939–1940?); "Gedanken zu William Paton: The Church and the New Order"; "Report on a Period of Study at the Union Theological Seminary in New York, 1930–1931," *NRS*, pp. 86–118; "Protestantism without Reformation" (1939), *NRS*, pp. 92–118. On the state cf. also Barmen V in A. C. Cochrane, *The Church's Confession under Hitler*, p. 241.
[35] Cf. above, Chapter IV.

for genuine worldliness, emancipation from self-justification, heteronomies, etc. "The commandment of Jesus Christ, the living Lord, sets creation free for the fulfilment of the law which is its own, that is to say, the law which is inherent in it by virtue of having its origin, its goal and its essence in Jesus Christ" (E, pp. 315 f.). The Lordship of Christ does not mean the lordship of the church over the world. The other mandates are freed by this proclamation to perform their own functions in their appropriate ways. If, e.g., the government should exceed its limits by exercising either too much or too little control,[36] the church has three possible ways of preserving the proper character of the mandates for the entering in of Christ: (1) to ask the state whether its actions are legitimate; (2) to aid the victims; (3) "to put a spoke in the wheel" (NRS, p. 225).[37]

Thus the church performs the important service of proclaiming the common Lord and of acting as a watchman. To the objection that worldly government can perform its service even without the encountering of the word of the church, Bonhoeffer replies: "When the Church perceives that a worldly order is on some few occasions possible without the preaching being heard (but still never without the existence of Jesus Christ), this will not impel her to disregard Christ, but it will elicit from her the full proclamation of the grace of the dominion of Christ. The unknown God will now be preached as the God who is known because he is revealed" (E, p. 296).[38]

A Critique of the Doctrine of the Mandates. The most important critique of Bonhoeffer's doctrine of the mandates is that of Karl Barth.[39] He regards Bonhoeffer's doctrine as an important step forward compared with the theologies of the order of creation and

---

[36] This is no less a temptation for the other mandates, especially for the church. But for Bonhoeffer it was mainly the government that misused its power.

[37] A similar argument will be found in E, pp. 387 f.

[38] Cf. also E, pp. 311, 313 f. On the church as whole, cf. "Barmen VI" in Ernst Wolf, *Barmen*, p. 150.

[39] *Church Dogmatics* III/4 ff. Barth deals in this passage with the theology of the orders as espoused by Brunner and Althaus. J. Moltmann is in partial agreement with this critique of Barth's; cf., above, pp. 92 f. and MW III, p. 63.

of natural law. This is because of its christological and biblical foundations. He is critical of Bonhoeffer's particular selection (it is too restricted) and of the all-pervasive hierarchical structure which he gives them. Bonhoeffer seems to attach more importance to authority than to the freedom even of the person at the bottom. The term "mandate" itself. which is almost identical with "commandment" and which imparts in advance a certain imperative coloring to these relationships, is also unsatisfactory.

The selection certainly has a biblical stamp and is typically Western.[40] Bonhoeffer is without doubt strongly influenced by the Lutheran doctrine of the orders. His intention is "to renew and to restore the old notion of the institution, the estate and the office" (*E*, p. 254). For this purpose he plans to write *Ethics* for the countries of the West.[41]

It is obvious that Bonhoeffer is very conservative in his attitude to government and authority, and Karl Barth's question, "Is the notion of the authority of some over others really more characteristic of the ethical event than that of the freedom of even the very lowest before the very highest?" (*Church Dogmatics* III, 4, p. 22), is perfectly justified. But Bonhoeffer has no intention of sanctioning the *status quo* in power structures. In fact, the mandate corrects and coordinates them (cf. *E*, pp. 255 ff. and *CD*, p. 225). Bonhoeffer uses the term "mandate" only for want of a better word. He might possibly have chosen "institution." [42] His cosmos of mandates seems to cause him problems, as is shown in his letter of January 23, 1944 (*LPP*, pp. 124 f.). He is concerned to find the place within the mandates for his "sphere of freedom," which seems to him to belong to the fullness of man. "Our Protestant (not Lutheran) Prussian world has been so dominated by the divine decrees, that it has allowed this sphere of freedom to be pushed into the background. It almost looks to-day as though the Church alone offers any prospect for the recovery of the sphere of freedom (art, education, friendship and play, 'aes-

[40] So J. Moltmann, in *MW* III, p. 63.
[41] Cf. *E*, pp. 23 f., as well as the title notes printed by E. Bethge in the editor's preface to *E*, p. X. Cf. also E. Bethge, "Dietrich Bonhoeffer—Der Mensch und sein Zeugnis," in *MW* II, p. 94.
[42] Cf. J. Moltmann, above, p. 22. Bonhoeffer actually uses the term "institution" in *E*, pp. 103 f., for church and state.

thetic existence') as Kierkegaard called it" (*LPP*, pp. 124 f.).
Bonhoeffer discovers here aspects of life which he can incorporate
into his cosmos of mandates only with obvious difficulty, but
which are certainly to be derived from the incarnation.[43] He only
raises the question whether they should be incorporated into the
church, and he clearly does not find the answer there. At any
rate, it shows that Bonhoeffer could not include the whole of
life in the mandates, although he tried to make them all-
embracing.

It is true that Bonhoeffer is convinced that the mandates, attested as they are by the Bible, are blessed with mission and
promise. They seem to have "their type in the celestial world" (*E*,
p. 295).[44] "Amid the changes of all historical institutions these
divine mandates continue until the end of the world" (*E*, p. 294).
So he attempts to construct an ethic here and now for the West.
He accepts "historically realized structures of contemporary life"
for the social formulation of a certain phase and grants them a
relative imperative character. Yet he would be "misunderstood
were one to read into the teaching of the mandates a revelation-
theological ideal—typical system of social order." [45] He is not
concerned with the orders for their own sake; still less does he
seek to create privileges for earthly relationships. Rather, he tries
to prove the unity of God and the world, and to incorporate them
into the dominion of Christ "with obedience in faith" (*E*, p. 322).
That is why I can agree with Ernst Wolf's judgment when he
says: " 'Mandate' leads him to accept institutions as tasks to be
given shape by concrete decisions." [46]

This is confirmed by Bonhoeffer's answer to his own question:
"But is not all responsible action in one's own calling confined
within inviolable limits by the law of God as it is revealed in the
ten commandments as well as by divine mandates of marriage,
labour and government?" His answer is: "Yet is it precisely responsible action which will not separate this law from its Giver"

[43] Cf. Chapter VI, section 3.
[44] He does not mention any type for the church.
[45] J. Moltmann, in *MW* III, p. 63.
[46] Ernst Wolf, " 'Trinitarische' oder 'christologische' Begründung des Rechts?"
in *Recht und Institution, Glaube und Forschung* 9 (Witten: Lutherverlag,
1956), p. 27.

(*E*, pp. 228 f.).[47] Thus, in the last analysis, freedom is included within the mandates, and by analogy it is possible to say this about Bonhoeffer's doctrine of the mandates: "So the institution loses its character of statically understood privilege and becomes involved in movement, in contingency, in occurrence, determined by the decisions of faith and obedience." [48]

The mandates exist only "for the sake and purpose of Christ" (*E*, p. 284). They are an expression of the dominion of Christ and have a major role to play in the realm of the penultimate.

VII.

Summary and Conclusion

I have attempted to illustrate the relationship between Christology and ethics in Bonhoeffer from specific ethical topics. As Bonhoeffer saw it, the all-important question is: What is the source of our self-knowledge, such as it is, our knowledge of our reality, our life and our being, and from whence do we receive the commandment? He contemplates God, man, and all created reality alike in the light of the revelatory act of God in Jesus Christ, i.e., in the light of the incarnation, cross, and resurrection. In this act man and the world are judged and reconciled, and this Lord Jesus *is* the universal Lord over all reality. This Lordship is hidden because it is the Lordship of the Crucified Lord who is still to come again, and cannot be derived from empirical reality. For all that, it is nonetheless real, even if for us here and now it is a matter of faith and proclamation. Although the night is not yet passed, the day is at hand (*E*, pp. 16 f.) and the world must surely, whether it knows about its Lord or not, be treated as though it were subject to the dominion of Jesus Christ. With this

[47] Cf. also *CD*, pp. 239 f. (quoted above, p. 135).
[48] Ernst Wolf, in *EvTh* 9 (1949–1950), p. 137.

we may compare the observation of Hanfried Müller: "In this connection it is immaterial for Bonhoeffer, who always believed in the universality of God's grace, whether the world is aware of it or not, so far as its actions are concerned. Since we Christians are aware of the emancipation of the world we must treat it as a free world—that is what matters, and matters even more in the moment when this natural world is recognized as having come 'of age' and as possessing a relative autonomy of its own." [1] Bonhoeffer is bound to be critical of any scheme of ethics which starts from a "concept of reality which underlies the positivistic ethic, the meretricious ethic of the empirically verifiable" (*E*, p. 60). For baptism occurs only after birth, so that the Christian is human before he becomes a Christian. And he is equally critical of any kind of philosophical ethics.[2] Such schemes can only lead to abstractions.

The commandment comes only from the God who became man in Jesus Christ and who in him has already fulfilled the commandment. Alongside him there are no "other events and powers, figures and truths" which are acceptable "as God's revelation." [3] With this we may compare another passage from Bonhoeffer himself: [4] "There are Christians who say: 'there are other things *alongside* their faith in God (which they will never give up), such as the world, the state, their work, their families, science, art and nature. All these have a legitimate place of their own. God says nothing has any right of its own alongside of him—only under him. Anything we put alongside of God is an idol" (*GS* IV, p. 603). Natural law, historical events, institutions remain undoubtedly as phenomena but not as ideologies and consequently do not have the last word.[5] There are no "areas in our

[1] Hanfried Müller, *Von der Kirche zur Welt* (Hamburg-Bergstedt: Herbert Reich, 1961), pp. 315 f.
[2] On this point, as well as on the whole concluding summary, cf. Wolfgang Trillhaas, *Ethik* 2 (rev. ed.; Berlin: Töpelmann, 1956), pp. 1 ff., especially pp. 6 f., 13 f.
[3] From Barmen I; trans. in A. C. Cochrane, *The Church's Confession under Hitler*, p. 239.
[4] "Die erste Tafel der zehn Worte" ("The First Table of the Decalogue"), June–July, 1944 (Tegel), GS IV, pp. 597–612.
[5] The wording of the above is modeled on Ernst Wolf, "Libertas christiana," in Hans Emil Weber and Ernst Wolf, *Gerechtigkeit und Freiheit*, ThEx, N.F. 18 (Munich: C. Kaiser, 1949), p. 31, cf. Bonhoeffer, *E*, pp. 302 f.

life in which we would not belong to Jesus Christ, but to other lords." [6]

As I have already sought to show from the quotations, Bonhoeffer's *Ethics* is really an expansion of the theology of the Barmen Declaration. He cannot regard ethics as an independent discipline alongside dogmatics, but he can say with Karl Barth: "Its matter is the Word and work of God in Jesus Christ, in which the right action of man has already been performed and therefore only waits to be confirmed by our action." [7] This shows that ethics is not a possibility for man on his own. And, as Bonhoeffer is aware, this presupposes a decision of faith: "The point of departure for Christian ethics is not the reality of one's own self, or the reality of the world; nor is it the reality of standards and values. It is the reality of God as He reveals Himself in Jesus Christ. It is fair to begin by demanding assent to this proposition of anyone who wishes to concern himself with the problem of Christian ethic. It poses the ultimate and crucial question of the reality which we mean to reckon with in our lives, whether it is to be the reality of the revelational word of God or earthly imperfections, whether it is to be resurrection or death" (*E*, pp. 56 f.).

This means that the world does not have to be Christianized. Instead, the dominion of Christ over all realms frees everything for its own proper concern, for genuine worldliness. Bonhoeffer's *Ethics* does not hover above reality but seems at least to make the commandment of God count in modern Western civilization. In the light of the revelation in Christ, concrete, historical reality, the place of the obedience of faith, is drawn to meditate upon the commandment. And, as I see it, it is through this that Bonhoeffer gives concrete directions for a life in Christian liberty, apart from the casuistry of an ethic based on duty but free from inwardness and from a preoccupation with individual sanctification, free for the formation of the world here and now.

[6] From Barmen II, quoted from A. C. Cochrane, *The Church's Confession under Hitler*, p. 240.
[7] *Church Dogmatics* II/2 (1957), p. 543.

INDEX

Abraham, 50

Act, 59, 67; sociology of, 47-53

Act and Being (Bonhoeffer), 15, 21, 27n., 47-51 passim, 77, 98, 102, 104, 106, 107, 120, 121, 125n., 126n.

Adam, Adamite man, 39-42, 43, 104, 125, 127, 131

Althaus, 92, 146n.

Analogia relationis, 53-55

Aquinas, Thomas, 29, 39

Aristotle, Aristotelianism, 29, 50, 51

Arseniev, 42

"Authentic worldliness," 16, 65-67; *see also* Christ, dominion of

Authority, 147; leader vs. office, 144

Barcelona lecture (Bonhoeffer), 99, 111, 127, 135

Barmen (Wolf), 146n.

Barmen Declaration, 119n., 145n., 146n., 150n., 151

Barth, Karl, 11, 12, 14, 23n., 35, 48, 50n., 59n., 82, 97, 99, 100, 102, 105n., 107n., 112n., 119n., 128n., 133n., 135n., 138n., 141n., 142, 144n., 151; act vs. being, 47; and *analogia relationis*, 55; Bonhoeffer and, 15n., 22; doctrine of revelation, 15n.; on the mandates, 26, 85, 92-93, 146-147; "special ethics," 52, 73; trinitarianism, 52-53

Being, 59, 67; sociology of, 47-53; theological concepts of, 47; *see also* *Act and Being*; "Being for others"

"Being for others," 11, 14, 86, 106, 143; Christological basis of, 16, 44-47; *see also* Deputyship

Berlin, University of, 47n.

Berlin School, 24

Bethel Confession, 123n.

Bethge, Eberhard, 99, 107n., 110n., 112n., 147n.

Bible, ethical directions of, 135-137; and mandates, 148

Biblical concepts, nonreligious interpretation of, 13-14, 15

Bollnow, O. F., 139n.

Bonhoeffer, Dietrich, development of thought, 56; and Luther's "primary powers," 88-89 (*see also* Luther); martyrdom of, 12; problems in interpretation of, 15-17, 97-98; relation to Barth, 52-53, 100n.; *see also* titles of books

Bonhoeffer colloquium (Union Theological Seminary), 14

Brunner, Emil, 92, 146n.

Buber, Martin, 29, 33, 36; on Kierkegaard's personalism, 34; principle of relationship, 54n.

Bultmann, Rudolf, 37n., 40, 48; act vs. being, 47

Center, concept of, 127-133, 137, 138, 139; *see also* Christ

Christ, as center, 130, 137; as community, 56; deputyship (vicarious action) of, 42-47, 56, 64-67, 143; dominion of, 16, 64-71, 112, 119-

153

Index

146-147; basis of, 21-23, 75, 140-142, 148; bearers of, 143-144; and Christ, 84, 139, 144-146, 149; deputyship and, 110n., flexibility of concept, 78; and freedom, 147, 149; functions of, 89-92; interrelationship of, 86-89, 142-143; legitimization of divine authority, 141-142; limitations of, 93-94; and Luther's "primary powers," 73-74; revelation of, to man, 70; scope of, 84-85, 148; transcendent order of reality, 77-79; see also Church; Culture; Government; Labor; Marriage

Marcionism, 34

Marriage, mandate of, 22, 64, 72, 76, 78, 84, 140; functions, 90, 144

Meuss, Gisela, 97n., 107n., 143n.

Ministry (office), doctrine of, 57-58, 120-121, 141, 143n.

Moltmann, Jürgen, 15, 16, 97, 98n., 99n., 100n., 102, 103, 105n., 113, 119n., 121, 124n., 131n., 138n., 140-148 passim

Monad concept, 104n.

Moses, farewell song of, 46-47

Müller, Hanfried, 15n., 107, 150

"Natural" life, 81-82

Nature, 112, 116

New humanity, new man, 42-46, 124-133

Nietzsche, Friedrich, 99, 138n.

No Rusty Swords (Bonhoeffer), 69, 70, 79, 100n., 112n., 115n., 120, 125n., 127, 134-137, 143n., 144, 145n., 146

Obedience in faith, 73, 92, 126, 148; mandates and, 75

Office, *see* Ministry

Ontology, 21, 49; confusion with kerygma, 28

Orders, doctrine of, 84, 146n., 147; *see also* Creation; Preservation

Ortega y Gasset, 138n.

"Outline for a Book" (*LPP*), 11, 14, 110n.

Pannenberg, W., 102

Paul, 40, 135

Penultimate, 149; period of, 79-84, 87, 126

Peregrinatio (Wolf), 23n., 74n., 75n., 77n., 82n., 89n., 118n., 137n., 143n.

Permission, concept of, 137-139

Person, 100; Christian concept of, 31, 101-103; collective person, 42, 103; deputyship and, 45; in Kant, 30; in Kierkegaard, 102n.; in Luther, 103; whole person, 116, 124-125; *see also* Man

Personalism, 125; in Bonhoeffer, 32-38; in Buber, 33-34; foundation of, 104; in Gloege, 49; in Gogarten, 34-35, 102; and guilt, 109; in Kierkegaard, 33-34; and sociality, 36-38; theological, 29

Personality, 22; "collective personality," 37; epistemological doctrine of, 29; individual vs. collective, 100; and I-Thou relationship, 85; metaphysical scheme and, 29-30; and sociality, 36-38; structures of, 38

Political Ethics (Gogarten), 34n.

Politik zwischen Dämon und Gott (Künneth), 72n.

Positivism, 67

Prayer, in religionless world, 13

Prenter, Regin, 15n., 100n., 111n., 126n., 131n.

Presence of Eternity, The (Bultmann), 37n.

Preservation, order of, 72, 79-80, 123, 139-140

Privilege, 138n.

Race, *see* Human race

Ranke, 27

Reality, 22, 28, 59-64, 67-69, 77, 87; Christ and, 68-69, 71, 141; and ethics, 70, 111-124, 151; mandates and, 142-143; meaning of, 59; messianic character of, 61; as penultimate, 122-124; and personalism, 60; and resurrection, 118-119; structures of, 115-118; unity of, 62-64; *see also* Deputyship

BIBLICAL REFERENCES

42353